Remembering BEautiful YOU

111 Days of
Sacred Healing

Rachelle Rose Kinney

WESTBOW
P R E S S®
A DIVISION OF THOMAS NELSON
& ZONDERVAN

This book is a work of non-fiction. Unless otherwise noted, the author and the publisher make no explicit guarantees as to the accuracy of the information contained in this book and in some cases, names of people and places have been altered to protect their privacy.

WestBow Press books may be ordered through booksellers or by contacting:

WestBow Press
A Division of Thomas Nelson & Zondervan
1663 Liberty Drive
Bloomington, IN 47403
www.westbowpress.com
1 (866) 928-1240

Because of the dynamic nature of the Internet, any web addresses or links contained in this book may have changed since publication and may no longer be valid. The views expressed in this work are solely those of the author and do not necessarily reflect the views of the publisher, and the publisher hereby disclaims any responsibility for them.

Any people depicted in stock imagery provided by Getty Images are models, and such images are being used for illustrative purposes only.
Certain stock imagery © Getty Images.

Interior Image Credit: Kathryn Letson

Scripture quotations marked (NLT) are taken from the Holy Bible, New Living Translation, copyright ©1996, 2004, 2015 by Tyndale House Foundation. Used by permission of Tyndale House Publishers, a Division of Tyndale House Ministries, Carol Stream, Illinois 60188. All rights reserved.

Scripture quotations marked (NIV) are taken from the Holy Bible, New International Version®, NIV®. Copyright © 1973, 1978, 1984, 2011 by Biblica, Inc.™ Used by permission of Zondervan. All rights reserved worldwide. www.zondervan.com The "NIV" and "New International Version" are trademarks registered in the United States Patent and Trademark Office by Biblica, Inc.™

Scripture marked (NKJV) taken from the New King James Version®. Copyright © 1982 by Thomas Nelson. Used by permission. All rights reserved.

Scripture quotations marked (ESV) are from The ESV® Bible (The Holy Bible, English Standard Version®), copyright © 2001 by Crossway, a publishing ministry of Good News Publishers. Used by permission. All rights reserved.

ISBN: 978-1-9736-9604-9 (sc)
ISBN: 978-1-9736-9603-2 (hc)
ISBN: 978-1-9736-9605-6 (e)

Library of Congress Control Number: 2020912303

Print information available on the last page.

WestBow Press rev. date: 07/15/2020

I dedicate this book to all who undertake the healing and inner work necessary for restoration. I am with you in spirit and honor you for the blessing you are!

In loving memory of my mother, Nina Arnelle Swanson, who helped to pioneer Restorative Justice in Minnesota. The programs she wrote and took to the prisons, added a spirituality aspect that was so greatly needed for true restoration. I honor her legacy and hope to carry on her mantle by allowing God to work through me to help people heal and restore into who they were born to be.

Acknowledgments

I want to give a special thank-you to Marjorie Cole, who ensured the completion of this book with her support and by facilitating my deliverance from the lies that paralyzed me. She helped me to uncover generational trauma that went back to the time of my ancestors. I cannot express enough my gratitude and respect for this beautiful woman of God. Her work in deliverance ministry has helped thousands realize the truth of who they are and helped set them free.

Marjorie can be found at www.liferecovery.com

Introduction

We are living in amazing times as God is dismantling all destructive programming imposed on the minds of humanity. Living under the influence of these programs has caused so much chaos and trauma. There is historical, generational, and personal trauma that is impacting the way we live life. As more people wake up spiritually, the need for healing is crucial. These deep-seeded programs that keep us in bondage must be recognized so that our God-given, true nature can emerge. We are beings of God's love and light. Anything not aligned with God's love is against the intended design of humanity and therefore will cause discord. Just like a fish must live in water according to its nature, we to need to live according to the nature God designed for us.

Sacred healing means God is guiding the process and orchestrating exactly what we need to process through past hurts, traumas, and grief that may cause destructive emotions to get trapped in our bodies. Because emotion is energy in motion and is meant to be processed and released, when it does not get processed in a healthy way it causes discord and dis-ease. Trapped emotion is unprocessed trauma that does not get released in some way, and it causes problems in the body and the mind. It can form into matter in the cells and impede the body's natural processes. Every physical ailment begins in spirit (the unseen) and then manifests in the physical. The ones we inherited begin in this way with family members who came before us, and it is passed through DNA tags. Epigenetic inheritance studies* have made findings that go against the idea that inheritance happens only through the DNA code that passes from parent to offspring. It means that a parent's experiences, in the form of epigenetic tags, can be passed down to future generations. These can be generational blessings or curses. In psychology, they are called "angels in the nursery" or "ghosts in the nursery." There are most likely many layers of old, unresolved family trauma in the form of an epigenetic tags, hidden within us and causing pain and dysfunction. I believe that if one family member's experiences can impact our DNA in this way, then another family member can experience a healing or resolve the trauma that caused the shift in DNA, and that could be imparted in the same way to heal the entire family line. With each healing, the epigenetic tag falls away for many. This is an aspect of the gospel message. Jesus overcame these things to make it possible for us to overcome generational traumas as well. When Jesus incarnated on Earth, there were no humans that did not have corrupted DNA due to trauma. He was sent into the Earth with the perfect divine DNA intact. We are all spiritually or energetically connected through electromagnetic fields, so when one person has an experience it literally affects everyone through those invisible fields. Jesus purpose was to make it possible for humanity to heal the DNA corruption we all inherited. He was literally the only one who could do this since he had his perfect DNA intact. Incarnating as a human and keeping his divine DNA intact by living in accordance with love as we were designed to live, he made it possible for everyone to heal their DNA. Through his act of overcoming, we now can overcome this dilemma and restore our DNA to the original divine blueprint. Jesus imparted this gift to us spiritually. All things can be healed through Christ, which is the absolute spiritual truth of all things. We were meant to live in loving harmony with God and all of God's creations through the living, active force of God's love.

*Epigenetic inheritance studies: Icahn School of Medicine at Mount Sinai, Rachel Yehuda PhD

This book is designed to help initiate the restoration process described in 1 Peter 5:10 NIV: "And the God of all grace, who called you to his eternal glory in Christ, after you have suffered a little while, will himself restore you and make you strong, firm and steadfast." I believe that the suffering spoken of in this verse is the tussle we go through with our old self as we are healing and learning healthier ways of living. Knowing that some of these traits of our old self are inherited and embedded into our genetic makeup, it makes sense there would be some suffering as we seek deliverance. The old self dies hard at times, and this may feel like suffering as the false ego is being dissolved so that our innate, God-given, true nature can emerge. It is a restoration right down to a cellular level.

The purpose of this book is as follows.

- Assist in a spiritual awakening
- Help heal and release personal trauma
- Help release the inherited generational trauma of our ancestors
- Help receive deliverance from strongholds and destructive programming of the mind
- Allow God to fully restore us
- Teach readers how to live in spirit and truth by utilizing the armor of God

We know from the Gospel message that when we accept Christ into our hearts, we have access to an amazing, divine gift. Jesus incarnated to make it possible for humanity to have access to the Holy Spirit. Jesus's death and resurrection overcame the prior limits that hindered humanity from healing. As we heal and restore, this mystery will begin to make more sense. Jesus reveals more and more of himself to us as we are ready to comprehend.

This book is a tool to help facilitate the healing and restoration process that God ultimately brings forth.

Here are some tips to follow while going through your sacred healing.

- Pick a time of the day devoted to your meditation. Always begin in prayer.
- Read the daily scripture readings. The Bible is alive and active and works in us exactly as we need it to for the deepest healing.

- Find support! We all need a support system in life, especially during a healing journey.
- Keep an open mind to how Holy Spirit is guiding you. Trust God to orchestrate all you need.
- Be willing to honestly examine yourself and make changes in your thinking. Be mindful that God will bring up situations and experiences in your daily life that will bring opportunities to grow.
- Trust God's timing and do not feel rushed to get through your process of healing in a certain time frame.
- Allow yourself days to take a break and rest when it is needed.
- The meditations are based on the Armor of God. Look for the icon for that day and keep the image in your mind to help you remember the daily affirmation.

God bless you as you walk the path of remembering who you are in Christ!

With love,
Rachelle

Prayer to Initiate Sacred Healing

Our God in Heaven,

I thank you for leading me into this journey of sacred healing. I recognize my ways of living do not always align with who you made me to be. I want to thrive and live a joyous life as the person you designed, not the person the world has told me to be. I ask for deliverance from all that hinders your perfect will for me. I open my heart now to your truth and your love. Please guide me every step of the way as I learn, heal, and restore into who I am in you, Lord, so I can be a conduit for your powerful love to spread on Earth.

I know you sent Jesus to guide us all into love and peace. He laid down his life to set us free. He lived his life for us to know the depth of your love for us and so we could know the truth of who we are and the power we have when we are connected to you. Jesus imparted a gift to us that makes it possible for us to heal fully and restore into who we were meant to be. I receive this gift into my heart. I now accept Jesus as my teacher, my Lord, and my Savior. Show me the way and lead me in everything I think, say, and do.

I pray this in Jesus's name, amen.

For God so loved the world, that he gave his only Son, that whoever believes in him should not perish but have eternal life. (John 3:16 ESV)

DAY 1

Affirmation

I am worthy of healing.
I have faith in God to show me the way.

Oh, beautiful you, with your sweet smile
shining right through your pain,
still loving,
still caring,
still kind and true
to everyone except beautiful you.

Meditation

Let us start this journey with a leap of faith, consciously deciding to relinquish control and place our lives into the safe hands of our loving God and Creator. Feeling powerless over life can be a scary prospect if we do not have faith that God is helping us along. When we see life as a partnership with the all-knowing, omnipresent God, we can let go and be in the present moment. It is like the difference between using a GPS to get somewhere we have never been and trying to get there with no directions. A GPS sees everything from road conditions to the quickest route. It has a bird's-eye view, and so does God. We can trust that we will be shown all that we need to know in perfect timing.

God is love, literally. Love is a powerful force of creation that has no limits. Humankind is made in God's image, so therefore we are love. We are a manifestation of God's love in physical form and a conduit for his love to be expressed on earth in vast and creative ways. That is why we were created. We are truly intended to be the light of the world. God's love and light can shine through us if we receive him in our hearts. We have been given free will to make choices, yet if we want a life of peace and joy, we are wise to seek his will for us and not rely on our own understanding. When we seek first the kingdom of God, all we need is given to us. May we have faith that all things work for the good of those who love God. May we take comfort in his eagerness to help us be fulfilled and prosper in every way.

In Jesus's name, amen.
Daily reading: Proverbs 3:5–6

DAY 2

Affirmation

At my very core, I am love.
I freely give love, and it comes back to me tenfold.

Love, please come and find me
Exactly where I am.
I am hiding under shattered dreams.
Come catch me if you can.
Fill me up with comfort
So I, in turn, can be
The one who comes to find you.
For there I will find me.

Meditation

Let us reach out for the love we need. Many of us have grown up with a distorted definition of love. We have suffered much heartache and confusion, which has led to us unconsciously closing off our hearts to receiving love. God's essence of love pervades all of creation and truly is within each of us. It is within our hearts that God's powerful love resides, and it is activated through opening our hearts to giving and receiving love. That is how we connect with God. Once we do this, we will begin to heal. When we go through trauma, it is often unprocessed, and the memories of the trauma are held in our bodies. Our God-given, true nature is the image and likeness of God; anything not aligned with love brings forth discord within our bodies and our lives. When we chose to abide in God as we are intended to, God's love and essence fills us and flows through us. The essence of God's love can heal us from anything. The work must be done in our thought life for any real outward change in our lives. Our thoughts need to align with God's love if we are to live as who we truly are. We must be diligent about adjusting our thinking. Let us pray daily for God's truth to be revealed to us. God's love heals all things; may we love God, one another, and ourselves with all our hearts so we can restore the original divine blueprint of humanity that God intended for us.

In Jesus's name, amen.
Daily reading: 1 Peter 4:8 and Romans 8:28

DAY 3

Affirmation

*I am honest with myself and others about my physical,
emotional, mental, and spiritual needs.*

Feeling so alone,
Help so hard to find,
Desperate thoughts of loneliness
Trapped within my mind.
Suddenly I'm halted as
A voice inside me pleads:
*You are not ever alone—
just ask for what you need!*

Meditation

Let us strive toward living in truth and expressing our needs openly to ourselves and others. We all have them! However, often our needs are not so obvious and require some contemplation. Living in truth is about being honest with where we are at and looking deeply at our true intentions before we act. We must always act from a place of truth and love. This can be hard for those of us who have lived for so long pretending all is well. The fear of judgment and judgment of ourselves, especially with mental health issues, may trigger us to go into denial.

Let us be careful not to fall into believing the stigmas and falsehoods that keep us in a place of shame. We must strive to honor the truth of where we are for any true and lasting healing to take place. We may not like how things feel now, but it is when we see and accept reality that true healing is set in motion. We do not need to live in the illusion of isolation any longer. We can share from our hearts with God and those in our inner circle what is truly going on with us. We were born and designed to live interdependently with other humans because God loves us through people. Even if our circle is small, let us find that one person who feels safe to be open with. As intimidating as it may feel, let us break through the barrier of our silence to speak our truth and voice our needs. Let us courageously reach out for the love and support we all need and deserve.

In Jesus's name, amen.
Daily reading: Ephesians 4:25

DAY 4

Affirmation

I surround myself with positive people.
I protect my mind by setting healthy boundaries.

My spirit flies high over the mountains
As the rain becomes heavy on my wings.
A thunderous storm is coming.
This power is too much for me;
I must seek shelter.

Meditation

Let us seek shelter from those who dampen our spirits and drain our energy. The stress brought on by people who are angry, negative, or unkind is very damaging. It not only hurts us emotionally but also makes us physically sick. When we have dealt with these types of people in our everyday lives for a prolonged period, we may not even realize the impact it is having on us. This is especially true if we grew up in a dysfunctional family where shame and judgment were instilled in us from an early age. We may even believe we deserve or cause the mistreatment from others, or that we are just too sensitive. Those are lies! When we are young, we have limited options, but as adults, let us ask ourselves, "Is there someone in my life who is negatively impacting my well-being?" We are on a path of restoring ourselves and healing from the impact of growing up in a world that tells us lies. It is time to love ourselves enough to break free from those who hurt us. Protecting our minds from continual stress is our right and responsibility. Even if there are negative people in our lives whom we have no choice but to deal with, we can begin to set boundaries to protect ourselves. We can pray for the healing of these people and for our own spiritual protection. Let us take at least one small step to begin setting ourselves free from negative influences.

In Jesus's name, amen.
Daily reading: 1 John 5:19 and 1 John 4:4

DAY 5

Affirmation

Beautiful music tunes my body, mind, and spirit.

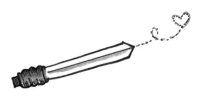

Music flows into deep places.
In hidden spots it finds
Healing hearts, calming nerves,
Hushing boisterous minds.
The beat carries magic—
The antidote of ails—
Leading us to happy times
And smoothing out our trails.

Meditation

Let us indulge in the sweet gift of music. In our busy minds, it can be difficult to be in the moment and simply enjoy a simple song. Music is such a healing force. It can help us find balance and joy in a hectic world. Our brains resonate to frequencies; different thoughts send out different frequencies. When we have a lot of stress, our brains get out of harmony. Certain tones will tune our brain waves and even get our cells resonating in harmony with love. It is okay to let go and enjoy this beautiful gift. The vibrations of certain music resonate deep within our beings, balancing and harmonizing us. This was known even in ancient times. Music has been a main aspect of praise and worship, rituals, festivals, and ceremonies since the beginning of time. God uses music to heal us and to create beauty. Humming is another way to use musical tones to balance ourselves. Each note on the musical scale harmonizes with the different centers in our bodies. When these centers are balanced and harmonizing with one another, it is like beautiful music flowing in our lives. We can go within our hearts, feel what we are needing, and allow music to activate healing. There are many wonderful musicians, and it is no coincidence that so many people were blessed with this gift to share. Let us use the healing power of music each day.

In Jesus's name, amen.
Daily reading: 2 Chronicles 5:13 and 1 Samuel 16:23

DAY 6

Affirmation

*I am healing at a perfect pace. I walk in peace
as I trust in God's divine timing.*

Slow and steady.
Like a raindrop on a pond
slowly ripples out,
I too shall slowly heal,
One drop at a time.

Meditation

Let us be patient and gentle with ourselves, taking time for rest and knowing that the process of transformation happens at a pace that is perfectly what we need. Time heals many things, and many things only time can heal. When we set the intention of walking a path of healing, progress is sure to follow. We can practice walking in peace by allowing time each day to be still and quiet, calming our minds through breathing. Healing is more about being than doing. Many times, we think we must be doing something to have results or progress. Yet restoring ourselves to our true nature is learning to be in the present moment and allowing God's love to flow in and through us to cleanse and rejuvenate us. When we can be still and focus on the essence of God's love flowing into us, it naturally restores all that is not aligned with peace and love. We are practicing letting go and letting God do for us what we could not do alone. Let us set aside time each day to do nothing but feel the connection we all have to God's love. We can breathe that love deep into our being and feel the powerful force of divine light transmuting all darkness within. This simple daily practice will profoundly accelerate our restoration process. So for now, nothing frantic, nothing hurried. Simply breathe and wait on the will of God to reveal itself.

In Jesus's name, amen.
Daily reading: Psalm 27:14 and Habakkuk 2:3

DAY 7

Affirmation

*I gently bring my thoughts back to love over and
over, until it becomes second nature.*

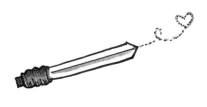

My precious thoughts are like magic keys
Unlocking possibilities.
I shall guard the ones that bring me peace,
And all the rest I shall release.

Meditation

Let us choose our thoughts well. Our thinking reflects what our hearts believe. This is particularly important because our hearts' beliefs carry amazing power. We are to use this for the good. While living in the kingdom of God, we have dominion over our life. In Romans 14:14 (NIV), Paul writes to the congregation, "I am convinced, being fully persuaded in the Lord Jesus, that nothing is unclean in itself but if anyone regards something as unclean then for him it is unclean." Our mind gives it the power. We have dominion over the earth, which is to say we have dominion over anything that is in the physical or is visible. Our minds and our beliefs give the power to produce the results our minds think it will produce. We are programmed to believe certain things produce certain results, and when we believe it in our hearts, then the results manifest. Once we allow that to sink in, and we know how much power our mind has, we can begin to shift our beliefs over to faith in this principle. Jesus expresses this in Mark 16:18 (NLT) when he says, "They will be able to handle snakes with safety, and if they drink anything poisonous, it won't hurt them. They will be able to place their hands on the sick, and they will be healed." When we use this principle with loving intent, we are in the kingdom of God. In the kingdom, we are connected into God and have power to manifest only that which is in harmony with God's love and goodness. Old beliefs lose their power over us as we begin to understand it was our own minds that ever gave them the power to manifest anything. In the next verses, Paul expresses the need to use this principle with love and consideration of others who do not yet realize this truth. He says in Romans 14:15–18 NIV, "If your brother or sister is distressed because of what you eat, you are no longer acting in love. Do not by your eating destroy someone for whom Christ died. Therefore, do not let what you know is good be spoken of as evil. For the kingdom of God is not a matter of eating and drinking, but of righteousness, peace and joy in the Holy Spirit, because anyone who serves Christ in this way is pleasing to God and receives human approval."

Let us remain vigilant about adjusting our thoughts to align with God's truth and love.

In Jesus's name, amen.

Daily reading: Philippians 4:8 and 2 Corinthians 10:5

DAY 8

Affirmation

*I bring all that is hidden in me to the light for healing. I am
slowly developing supportive and loving friendships.*

These secrets I'm keeping, nobody knows
the depth of my struggles are locked in my soul.
I'd give you the key and let you come in,
but I know I can't trust you; there's no one I can.
I've trusted before and seen where that's led.
Pictures are painted, then teardrops are shed.
So I go it alone, so safely I'll be,
No one quite knowing the truth about me.

Meditation

Let us begin to trust again as we seek out friendships with other loving souls. We all have a deep need to belong and to have support. When we have been deeply hurt in different relationships throughout our lives, we may close off our hearts to protect ourselves from more pain. Judgment from others in our past, betrayal, being bullied, abandonment—all these things can cause us to close off from trusting others. Many of us have an extremely hard time letting people into our lives due to these experiences. We can find support from other people who are walking similar paths. When we open and trust others with our deepest secrets, we release shame and bring any darkness within us into the light for healing. When we are carrying around shame from our past, we are unable to be our true selves with others. James 5:16 (NIV) says, "Therefore confess your sins to each other and pray for each other so that you may be healed. The prayer of a righteous person is powerful and effective." The wisdom behind this is that when we tell another about something that causes us shame or how we have lived against our true nature, we then bring it into the light and free ourselves. Confession is not about gaining forgiveness or redemption; it is meant to release us from the bondage of limiting shame and to demonstrate our spiritual understanding. May we begin to trust in others and share from our hearts what troubles us.

In Jesus's name, amen.
Daily reading: Romans 8:15 and James 5:16

DAY 9

Affirmation

*I face reality with assurance that all things work
for the good of those who love God.*

If I bury my head and cover my ears,
Will this painful truth disappear?
If I shove it away and pretend all is well,
Will I spare myself from the fear?

Meditation

Let us face this day with our eyes wide open. Do we have truths we are denying because we are afraid that accepting them will bring us pain? When we live in denial, we already are living with pain. Maybe we fear having to make difficult changes in our lives if we admit certain truths. Accepting difficult realities is the first step necessary in overcoming them. No amount of wishing can change certain things. We may need to have deep contemplation about where our lives are at and see where we have created realities with which we are not happy. Let us accept truth with courage and strength, knowing that we have the power to create the realities we desire when we live with love and in partnership with God.

How do we cope with painful realities? Psalm 55:22 (NIV) says, "Cast your cares on the Lord and he will sustain you, he will never let the righteous be shaken." We can have faith in God's love to sustain us always. When we are living in the righteousness of God's love, we are safe. Romans 8:28 (NKJV) teaches us, "And we know that all things work together for good to those who love God, to those who are the called according to his purpose." We can trust that when we love God and lift our worries up to the Creator, all things will be handled for the good. Not only that, but God will take every bad thing that has occurred and use it to create something beautiful and good. Let us keep our faith strong and our spiritual eyes wide open as we allow God to recreate a life of love and peace for us.

In Jesus's name, amen.
Daily reading: Romans 8:28 and Psalm 55:22

DAY 10

Affirmation

I am free as I live with just what I need, nothing in excess.

I walk this path with a light load,
Following the map of my heart,
Stopping along the way
To offer love to the weary.

Meditation

May we strive to live a simpler life by freeing ourselves of unneeded burdens. Excess comes in many forms. It can be material and physical, or it can be mental and emotional. Are we taking on too much work or responsibility? Do we have too many material belongings? Organizing helps us to feel our lives are more manageable. That includes organizing our schedules and our time to be more balanced. Let us begin to eliminate any excess we have in our lives. The lighter our load is, the more pleasant our journey will be. We can cut away the old with the sword of spirit, seeking to keep what resonates with our hearts and discarding all that is keeping us attached to false ego. When we attach to things or situations out of a desire to look a certain way, we are not living in alignment with our true selves. We can look beyond the surface at our intentions and motives. Then we can access what truly belongs in our lives and make sure it aligns with God. It can be a challenge for us to let go of things or people that we are used to, yet true freedom lies in living in the truth of who we are as divine beings of love. We can flip the trinity of body, mind, and spirit to spirit, mind, and body, allowing our spirits to be at the forefront to guide our minds rather than our physical, fleshly desires being in control. This is the intended design of humankind. May we find our inner peace as we allow God to guide our hearts and set free all that does not resonate with who we are in Christ.

In Jesus's name, amen.
Daily reading: Matthew 23:12

DAY 11

Affirmation

I have integrity in all that I do.

This job will be well done,
Though no one else will see.
I will do it for the sake of love,
Aiming to impress only me.

Meditation

Let us always strive to work with integrity. Leaving a job well done is good for our souls. Jesus says in his famous Sermon on the Mount, "Blessed are the meek; for they shall inherit the earth" (Matthew 5:5 ESV). By "inherit the earth," Jesus means having dominion over your entire outer experience. What manifests in our lives and bodies is a result of our mental attitude and subsequent thoughts. We must be meek to have this total dominion over our lives. To be meek as the Bible states is to have an attitude of openness to God's will for our lives. It means to be completely surrendered to God's plans and to have the meekness to know it is not our own power that manifests good in our lives but rather God's power through us. We must be open to new revelations that come to us and seek God's perfect plan. When we set intentions to work in spirit with honest integrity, we are living in harmony with God. Loving intentions send out God's love, and thus goodness will come back to us. It is a principle of the law of physics that like begets like. Flesh begets flesh, and spirit begets spirit. If our intentions are of the flesh, self-seeking, dishonest, or half-hearted, then what we send out is malicious, so we will be drawing those same types of experiences back to us. Living God's will does require a clear conscience to function for our highest good. Every aspect of our lives can be in loving harmony with God and our true selves when we practice integrity in all we do. No matter how small the task before us is, may we do it to the best of our abilities.

In Jesus's name, amen.
Daily reading: Hebrews 13:18 and Ephesians 4:32

DAY 12

Affirmation

I chose joy as my natural state of being.

This simple little feeling
Living within me,
Safe from the world and always there
Whenever I choose to feel it.
Oh, Joy, you wonderful friend of mine.

Meditation

Let us remember that joy resides within us as we abide in love. It is untouchable by outer circumstances and people. It is ours for the taking anytime we choose. Joy is our right as children of God! As we are restoring wellness and balance to our lives, joy is a key component to our healing. We can access this often by visualizing joyful memories or by stopping to enjoy the beauty that is everywhere. Even simply affirming, "I am joyful," will shift us into a higher vibration. We must remember that our thoughts and affirmations dictate what we manifest. We are powerful creators learning to use our words to call forth our hearts' desires. Desires of the heart are always based in love, and from love comes joy. We may wonder how we can be joyful in a time of sorrow. Joy and sorrow can happen simultaneously with each other; they balance each other. We may not always be happy because feelings come and go, but joy is a state of being that can be a constant in the background as we go through life. When we are practicing living under the law of love, we are abiding in the presence of God. The result will be joyful gratitude for life itself. Gratitude and awe spring forth as we heal and awaken to God working with and through us, and we finally realize we are creators our self! May we relish this gift of the spirit and affirm how worthy we are to have God's loving help each day!

In Jesus's name, amen.
Daily reading: Romans 15:13 and John 16:24

DAY 13

Affirmation

I send love to all of humanity like waves of light connecting us all.

You are my brother, my sister, my friend.
You are like me, and together we stand.
One world of spirits residing in peace,
Causing no harm as our fears we release.

Meditation

Let us send love to all of humanity. We have been conditioned to believe we are separate or different from other people, but this is a false teaching, an illusion that blinds us to the truth. The truth is we were created by God and come from the same original parents, and our roots trace back to the same family tree. We are all family here on this earth and are connected by genetic and energetic bonds. Only false beliefs separate us; we are all the same race, human beings. When we see the spiritual connection we have with everyone, we can heal from the illusion of separation. Simply closing our eyes for a few moments and picturing a ray of light wrapping around the world in a web and connecting all people can help trigger the remembrance of our true connection to all. This light is our collective love that intertwines through the hearts of all. This form of meditating connects us to God's healing love. At the core, what people truly need is the peace and contentment that love brings. Visualizing love and peace coming into us from God and then being sent out from our hearts to the entire world carries an essence that is so powerful, it can send out a healing force to the world and bring it right back to us. Let us help generate a more loving world by devoting a few moments every day to this practice.

In Jesus's name, amen.
Daily reading: 1 Corinthians 13:1–13 and Romans 12:4–5

DAY 14

Affirmation

I believe in the power of God's love to bring miracles into my life.

All I have seen and all I've been taught,
Like a rough draft of my life,
I must now edit and correct
To match who I truly am and all I wish to be.

Meditation

Let us begin to look carefully at our beliefs. All we have learned up to this point in our lives may not suit the people we truly are or who we were meant to be. Certain beliefs we may have been raised learning can be detrimental to our well-being. For many of us, this rings true as far as our religious upbringing. Beliefs that are based in fear or shame do not belong in our lives at all. Our beliefs hold so much power in shaping our lives. Having faith in something means we have total belief in it. This belief is the power that manifests in the outer world that which we believe. In the Bible, there are hundreds of scriptures that speak about the importance and power of faith. Our faith is said to have the power to create miracles.

Yet some beliefs hold us back. We can deprogram our minds from negative false beliefs that have a stronghold over our lives. Activating our innate ability to discern truth begins with dissolving the false ego. A few quiet moments every day to connect to our spirits and our hearts through prayer and meditation will begin opening our spiritual eyes. Recognizing ego-driven beliefs over love-driven beliefs will become very natural the more we open and live from our hearts, where God's love resides. Let us hold on dearly to only the beliefs that resonate with our loving hearts, honoring who we truly are. May we ask God to reveal the false beliefs we have unconsciously held in our hearts so we can release them.

In Jesus's name, amen.
Daily reading: Revelations 18:4

DAY 15

Affirmation

I am my own best friend.

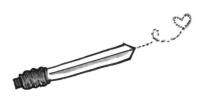

Hey, stranger who's always been here
And will be with me until the end.
I've been feeling sort of lonely.
Would you like to be my friend?

Meditation

Let us take time out each day to get to know our true selves better. The foundation for a happy life is built on loving God, others, and ourselves. Yet how can we love a stranger? Many of us have lived our lives for everyone else for so long that we do not know who we truly are. Yet loving and respecting ourselves is essential in order to give to others in a healthy way. The quality of our love for others improves greatly and is more fulfilling when we love ourselves. As we begin to look to our teacher within, the Holy Spirit, we cultivate more and more of our own true nature. We are in a time of tearing down the false ego self and building up the true, God-given self. When we do this and finally realize how amazing we are at our core, we in turn realize how amazing everyone is. When we get strong in that truth, we can go out in the world and withstand any negative comments or treatment from others without being impacted. We will be so solid in our love for ourselves and others that nothing can make that waver. We can look at those who are negative or cruel with new loving eyes, knowing they have not woken up to their true nature. Our love and nonreaction to them may push them closer to the truth. Romans 12:21 (NIV) says, "Do not be overcome by evil but overcome evil with good." Notice 12:21 and how the numbers get turned around. Yes, we can turn evil around with good! Just as truth overcomes lies, faith overcomes doubt, peace overcomes chaos, and spirit overcomes the flesh. The law of love is the highest law and overcomes all the lower laws of the universe. Let us keep our focus and spiritual eyes on that which overcomes, for that is our true nature in Christ.

In Jesus's name, amen.
Daily reading: Romans 12:21 and Mark 12:31

DAY 16

Affirmation

I use my breath to quiet my mind.

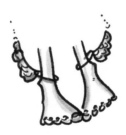

Like a record skipping,
So too is my mind
Spinning aimlessly,
Unable to proceed.
I must unplug,
Breathe ... breathe ...
Let the sweet silence sing its lullaby.
Be still, my weary head.

Meditation

Let us take time daily to unplug from everything long enough to quiet our minds. In this silence, we can take a deep breath and let go, practicing going with the flow of life rather than resisting. Inspiration, clarity, and wisdom flow smoothly through a quiet mind. With practice, quieting our minds becomes easier. Even amid turmoil, we can be calm in our hearts when we learn to take time each day to just be still. One way is to meditate through visualization. We can get comfortable either sitting or lying down with dim lights or candlelight and even some quiet gentle music. Then we can begin taking a few deep breaths and imagine blowing away all the noise from the day. With each breath, we relax our bodies more and more by focusing on the muscles that are tense and releasing them upon exhale. As we focus on slow deep breathing, with each inhale we can imagine drawing in God's love from the head to the feet. After a dozen breaths in and out, we can let go of the focus on our breath and allow our breathing to fall into a natural rhythm. We can bask in this state for as long as we like. While in this calm state, we are aligned with God. Let us use these moments to call forth and affirm our hearts' desires. We are the cocreators of our life. Let us rise to the higher realms through meditation and feel our loving connection to God.

In Jesus's name, amen.
Daily reading: Psalm 131:2 and Matthew 11:28–30

DAY 17

Affirmation

I am impeccable with my words.

If all the world was love,
And fear we never knew,
We'd never speak a hurtful word
Because love is always true.

Meditation

Let us speak only the language of love. Our words carry so much power that they can lift others up or tear them down. We can bless or curse people with our words. We already know that when we have belief in the words spoken to us, like a seed well-watered by our thoughts, it will begin to manifest in our lives for either the good or the bad. We therefore must be careful with both ourselves and others and speak only blessings of life and truth. Those who love and trust us take to heart the things we say; our words are seeds, and once in the heart, they manifest into the outer. If we say harmful things in anger or to hurt someone we love, the damage could be deadly. It can make a person believe lies about themselves that go against the truth of God. This is how sickness, disease, mental health issues, and self-hatred begin. Our loved ones should not have to guard their hearts against us; they should be free to be open with us and trust us to speak blessings over them.

We can look back and recognize where the words we have heard throughout our own lives have caused us to be cursed. These seeds planted in our hearts may have grown into so-called demons that torment us. We can now undo this damage by calling forth God's healing love to show us the inner work we must do to destroy these manifestations. Overcoming fears and old beliefs that have harmed us is the key to embodying love for ourselves and others. Pieces of our soul can get fragmented from unresolved trauma. When we experience trauma as children that never resolves, our minds form detrimental beliefs that can cause sickness, disease, and chaos in our lives. As we open and seek healing, old wounds will surface. Situations in our lives often trigger these wounds in us that stem from hidden hurts. This is our clue from God of the need for healing and deliverance from false beliefs. When a feeling of pain or defensiveness arises in us, we can set aside time to contemplate and trace the feeling back to the first time we ever felt it. When we reach the root of old wounds, we have a chance to release unhealed emotions by allowing the truth to come forth. What lie or false belief did this trauma convince us of? We can now look at the root belief that caused us to live against the truth of who we are. Let us use the power of spoken word to replace these lies with the truth that sets us free.

In Jesus's name, amen.

Daily reading: Proverbs 18:21, Mark 11:23, and Proverbs 12:18

The tongue has the power of life and death. (Proverbs 18:21 NIV)

DAY 18

Affirmation

*All aspects of my true self are emerging as God reveals
deeper spiritual understanding and truth.*

As I cultivate my true nature,
growth is slow and steady,
involving many shifts and changes.
I face the future reassured
as progress becomes visible,
knowing all else will follow.

Meditation

Let us celebrate our growth. Progress may be hard to see if we think in terms of yesterday. Let us look back a year and acknowledge how far we have come. Our ego-based reactions are dissolving, and our true, loving natures are now emerging to the forefront of our lives. When we embark on a journey of healing or self-growth, God moves and carries us along. All the tools and guidance we need are drawn to us when we seek to better ourselves. As we heal more and more, our egos begin to quiet as we see things through eyes of love. But at times the survival self is triggered, and we fall into old behaviors. We can tell when we are in harmony with our true selves if we look deeply at the intentions behind our behaviors. We want to be sure we are living, speaking, and behaving in accordance with our true self. When our intentions become unloving, we can gently bring ourselves back into harmony through meditation and prayer. When we step aside and take on the position of nonjudging observer of the self, we begin to see the depth of our conditioned minds. We have an opportunity to readjust our behaviors and break habitual tendencies that do not serve our highest good. As we diligently seek to live mindfully aware of our intentions, we can face the future reassured that we are making progress, and we can rejoice in this truth.

In Jesus's name, amen.
Daily reading: John 16:13 and 1 Peter 1:22

DAY 19

Affirmation

I quickly pick up on clues that I need to adjust my perceptions.

Whom have I been judging?
I must stop to reflect.
For when I think another is wrong,
Myself I must inspect.

Meditation

Let us take an honest look at ourselves. Clues can be found in our thoughts toward others. Whom are we judging harshly? Do we quickly come to assumptions about others that are negative? Maybe we are seeing something in others that reflect an image of ourselves. Are we negatively judging ourselves? Many of us have been shamed and wrongly judged during our childhoods. Sometimes we picked up right where they left off, and the shameful cycle of judging ourselves continues long after these people are gone from our lives.

We can gently remove this negativity by acknowledging and releasing any judgments we are holding on to and replacing them with the deeper truth and unconditional love. We can shift our immediate thoughts of judgment by reminding ourselves of deeper truths that are always based in love. The work is done during our meditations and put into practice as judgments arise in our minds. During quiet meditation, we can sit in silence and call forth the love of God to shift all our untrue mental conditioning back into the truth of love. We can call forth the opening of our spiritual eyes, the ones that see the hidden truth behind outward behaviors we witness in ourselves and others. We are preparing ourselves to have a keen eye for truth. For example, we may come across a person who is an attention seeker and deceives other in the quest for attention. This behavior may give rise to automatic negative judgments about this person, such as believing he is a vicious person. When our spiritual eyes open and begin to develop, we can look upon this person and see a different truth. We can see this person has low self-worth and that some trauma in his life caused him to suffer with torturous feelings of not being good enough. With this deeper truth, we can choose to help that person through being compassionate, or we can hurt him more with negative judgments. We can shift into compassion by seeing a deeper truth. Let us strive to mirror love and project compassion that is healing for all.

In Jesus's name, amen.

Daily reading: Luke 6:37 and Ephesians 4:29

Let all that you do
be done in love.
(1 Corinthians
16:14 ESV)

DAY 20

Affirmation

I am learning to set healthy boundaries in my life.

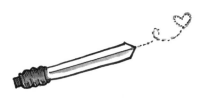

To love is not to fix you
Or care for all your needs.
It's not to take your worries on
Or every stress relieve.
To love is just to be there
To listen and to hold,
To offer you a warm embrace
When life is dark and cold.

Meditation

Let us remember that we are not responsible for the problems of others. To offer concern and support is a loving gesture, but to try to solve the issues of other people is not. It sends a message that they are not capable. Anything that drains our energy or infringes on our well-being must change. Therefore, if others put expectations on us that cause us to repeatedly put aside our own needs, we must set a boundary. If we remember that our needs must be met to give to others in a healthy way, we can stand firm in our decisions, even if others do not understand. We must remember that whatever we give our attention to governs our lives. When we allow others to pull our thoughts out of alignment with God's love and truth, we begin to serve two masters, so to speak. We must keep our spiritual eyes focused on God. Even when others try to push us into doing for them what they can do for themselves, let us lovingly set healthy boundaries for ourselves. That may be the most loving gift we can give.

In Jesus's name, amen.
Daily reading: Romans 16:17 and 2 Corinthians 6:14

DAY 21

Affirmation

In solitude, my deepest truth can be found.

Time alone to honor me,
To heal, to grow, to be okay.
To find my way
Alone.

Meditation

Let us remember to honor our healing process. At the beginning of any healing journey, there is a need to have regular periods of solitude. It is a path we must walk partly alone with God. This helps us filter through and process our feelings, understand them, and develop new and healthy ways of living. The helmet of salvation is about protecting our minds from anything that is not in alignment with the truth of God's love, which Jesus taught us about. If we have any unreleased grief inside of us, we may need to allow ourselves to feel it and get through it with no judgment. We may fear that crying or feeling pain is a sign of weakness or that we do not have it all together. But truly a person who can feel grief, even the hidden-away childhood grief, is a person who is healing. We may be dealing with current difficult situations that we have kept plugging through and not allowed ourselves time to process the tough emotions. It may be time to release the anger or hurt that was not allowed to come out before. This hidden pain manifests itself as disease if left inside of us. It is safe to allow the hurts to come up to the surface now and let the Holy Spirit deliver us at last. We must remember that the only way to the other side of grief is through it. Keeping our circle small for a period reduces the confusion of outside influences. Let us safeguard our minds and seek deliverance through God's love.

In Jesus's name, amen.
Daily reading: John 14:6 and Psalm 37:39

DAY 22

Affirmation

As I give my loving attention to others, my heart overflows with joy.

I will cradle you in my heart
and wrap you in my love.
I will be your gentle keeper
With help from up above.

Meditation

Let us remember our children, elders, and those in our lives who may be vulnerable, sick, or disadvantaged. Let us seek to care for them with joyful hearts. Who has been neglected that could use a little TLC? The most precious gift we can offer is our time and attention. Giving of ourselves this way is healing to our spirits. There is a powerful healing exchange that takes place between two people when one is giving with love and the other is receiving with gratitude. Our lives can get so full and busy that we feel that we do not have time for others. The truth is we can choose to set aside time and with conscious intent focus all our attention on those with whom we are present. This kind of focus is regenerative to our minds and can assist in realigning back into coherence with God. When we begin to feel overwhelmed and unable to be in the moment, we can release agitation easily with a deep breath and quick affirmation. It really can be as simple as that because all is a choice, and we have the power to choose at any given moment where we wish to focus our thoughts. Being fully present with the flow of life and loving exchanges with others are the way of God. May we embrace these new realities with open hearts and minds.

In Jesus's name, amen.
Daily reading: James 1:27

DAY 23

Affirmation

I am one with all of humanity.

I stepped into your shoes
and looked through your eyes.
I laughed your laughs
and cried your cries.
I rejoiced in your joys
and felt the aches of your pains.
And realized our spirits
were one in the same.

Meditation

Let us seek to be compassionate to others. We can understand the mistakes, struggles, disappointments, and hardships of everyone when we open our hearts and minds to the realization that we are all one. We have all come into this world as innocent beings of love and were born into lives that shaped the way we think, believe, and operate. The conditioning we were born into is not our fault; the way we were programmed to operate has been filled with so much distortion and untruths. Damage that has happened due to the nature of a fallen world is hidden from us until we wake up and finally realize that something is not quite right. The process of unraveling the mess of our upbringing takes time and effort. As we heal from the old way of living and begin to align with God's truth, we start to see all the intricate mind conditioning and its impact on us. At our very core, we are all loving beings. Some have awoken to this truth and healed; some are just awakening and beginning the healing journey. There is a lot to be processed and realigned. As we take up our own sacred healing, let us remember that we are all one in the same, just at different places and stages. Let us see with new loving eyes those who have hurt us in the past or continue to hurt us, knowing that under it all is a loving person who has been deceived. May we dissolve the false beliefs of separation and begin to see the truth of our connection to God and all humanity.

In Jesus's name, amen.
Daily reading: Ephesians 4:6

DAY 24

Affirmation

I send out waves of love through my smile.

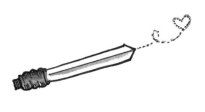

Your smiling face
Melts my pain
So I can face the world again.

Meditation

Let us remember how powerful a smile can be. A smile says so many sweet things in an instant. We can all remember a time when we felt down, and someone offered us such a genuine, heartfelt smile that our spirits instantly lifted. The power of God's healing love is sent out into the world as we abide in God's love and light. When we are open to the Holy Spirit flowing through us, we emanate God's love. Words are a small fraction of how we communicate. We can utilize this ability to transfer the power of love through the nonverbal communication of a smile. More is happening than our eyes can even see. We can make this a conscious action as we practice aligning our minds and thoughts with God. We are developing the mind of Christ as we do this. We can balance out negativity and create harmony with others. Let us smile at everyone we see no matter who it is. If that is all we did, it would truly be enough to make the world a happier place to be!

In Jesus's name, amen.
Daily reading: Hebrews 4:12

DAY 25

Affirmation

The light of God's love heals everything as I allow
the Holy Spirit to reveal truth to me.

The Great Teacher, once again disguised,
Has engulfed me in darkness and pain.
I will undergo this lesson with dignity.
I will search out the hidden truth
And bring it into the light,
Returning all to love.

Meditation

As we reflect on our lives, may we recognize where we may be holding onto pain to avoid a deeper truth. Are we using our pain or difficult situations to justify certain behaviors or habits that we feel benefit us? Could we be afraid to heal and make healthy changes because doing so would mean letting go of our crutches? We can bring all truth to the surface now and really contemplate what is serving our highest good and what is holding us back from being free to be who we naturally are. There are blessings that come from our hardships, and one of them is recognizing how we are manifesting our own difficulties by living against ourselves. Hardship reflects our thought life and habits. All pain and suffering can transform to love when we break free from denial or old conditioning and look in the face of truth. Programming of the mind can be so deeply ingrained that it can take a crisis for us to recognize it. Maybe we are holding on to bitterness over our struggles. Let us shift our perspective to observe truth so we can swiftly process through all the difficult feelings that cause us dis-ease. We can be grateful for all experiences that bring us into awareness of the outmoded thinking patterns that make us sick. We are only as sick as our secrets, so let us be honest with ourselves and begin the healing that follows. Truth leads us to love, and love heals all things and sets us free from all suffering!

In Jesus's name, amen.
Daily reading: John 8:32 and John 16:13

DAY 26

Affirmation

I am getting to know myself.

I know my worth and goodness.
This knowing is the key
That unlocks the door to freedom,
Awakening all my dreams.

Meditation

Let us remember that life responds to what we think of ourselves. Goodness is blocked when we do not feel deserving of it. We can remove these blocks as we recognize and change negative thought patterns we have developed. Maybe we did not grow up hearing how wonderful we truly are. Maybe we were told lies about ourselves that we have believed for many years. Let us look deep into our hearts and remind ourselves of the truth: that we are beautifully made in the image of the Creator. As we learn more and more how to live from a place of love, this truth of who we are is remembered. Our minds were designed to follow the guidance of our hearts, our divine guidance system where God speaks to us. Our hearts are always in the here-and-now moment, whereas our minds can take us back to the past or into the future. This serves a good purpose for planning and creating the life we desire, yet when we allow our minds to wander away with anxiety from the present moment, fragments of our souls can get scattered all over the place. We can call back all aspects of ourselves through prayer and start being mindful of staying in the present. Even when we contemplate memories to heal or grow, we can make it a practice to pray and affirm that our souls come back to us as we come back into the moment. Let us focus our thoughts upon our God-given, beautiful nature and affirm who we truly are in Christ.

In Jesus's name, amen.
Daily reading: Genesis 1:27

DAY 27

Affirmation

I lift my spirits as I engage with others.

This yearning washes through me,
Oceans of loneliness vast and deep
Drowning my spirit.

Meditation

Let us acknowledge our need for social interaction. Isolation can be instinctive when we are feeling down. This learned behavior is self-defeating. We can look at the root of why we isolate and see that it is based upon untrue beliefs and fears. When we fear judgment or have shame, we want to hide. When we have been hurt by others who judge us negatively, it can cause us to put up protective walls. We are now safe to come out of hiding! We have come far enough in our realization of the truth about who we are. We do not have to be doing wonderful to be around others. We can accept ourselves exactly where we are at and know that no matter where our lives are at, we are amazing, beautiful souls! Let us slowly break the old habit of isolating by seeking out others who are supportive and loving. When we push past the fear of social anxiety, we begin to see how beautiful it can be to share our life with others! Roman 14:19 (NKJV) says, "Therefore, let's keep on pursuing those things that bring peace and that lead to building up one another." The times when we are feeling our lowest are the times when we need others the most. When developing good healthy routines, let us be sure that making time for building up one another is a priority. We need and deserve loving relationships in our lives. Let us not fall into the habit of isolating.

In Jesus's name, amen.
Daily reading: 1 Thessalonians 5:11 and Ecclesiastes 4:9–12

DAY 28

Affirmation

I look within for the voice of God for answers and truth.

All the confusion,
People seeking truth,
Dazed by the magnitude of half-truths,
Distorted information.
Mental overload prevents discernment.
But all the while, the truth is right there,
Not outside of them.
It is within, encoded in their hearts,
Accessible through prayer.

Meditation

Let us decompress from all the information swirling around us by tuning in to our hearts and aligning with God's perspective. We can be still and quiet and allow gratefulness to fill our minds, thinking of the blessings all around us. Our true blessings are always based on love: our children's smiles when they accomplish something new, our friends' laughter, random acts of kindness we witness, happiness of others, and all the little things that warm our hearts. As we focus on these things our hearts fill with gladness, it is in that space that we find truth. God speaks to us through love. Our internal guidance system that God designed within us can discern what is of God and what is of fear or a remnant of some trauma. Truth will give us a sense of knowing and peace. Truth is based in divine love. Let us go within to seek truth through loving thoughts and prayers of gratitude, allowing the Holy Spirit to show us all we need to know. In this place, we will be shown what mindsets and strongholds we still need deliverance from. When an old, unhealthy thought or feeling arises in us, we can gently affirm the truth that God is handling everything for us and we are children of the Most High God, made holy in his image. Let us rest in this truth as the Holy Spirit purifies our hearts and renews our minds.

In Jesus's name, amen.
Daily reading: 1 Corinthians 13:2 and 1 Peter 4:10

DAY 29

Affirmation

My faith in God is my peace.

In the light,
I am free to be peaceful.
Even in darkness,
my peace rests with God.

Meditation

Let us not be discouraged when all seems well, and suddenly our lives take a dark turn. It is easy to find our inner peace when things around us are smooth and going in our favor. As we strive for growth in Christ, there will be disruptions to our peace. Things will go wrong at times, and others will let us down. We will think we have it all figured out, and then something will shake up our security. One thing that never has to falter is our peace. When we are allowing God to be our foundation in life, we can weather any storm. We can consciously decide which thoughts to dwell on. If we have the ability to think, we can be free! At times, our descents into darkness happen to help us wake up or realize that we are heading in the wrong direction. At other times, it may feel as if everything is falling apart when truly it is falling into place. God often intercedes in our lives for our good, but it takes a while for it to all make sense. Those who are truly diligent about seeking deliverance from all that hinders who they are in Christ will be persecuted internally as the old self is dissolving. The good news is that the persecution is coming from none other than ourselves and the old, conditioned, false self. That means when we feel the most persecuted, we are in a time of great growth and radical healing. Jesus says in Matthew 5:10 (NKJV), "Blessed are those that are persecuted for righteousness sake, for theirs is the kingdom of Heaven." As we seek right thinking and to live in God's righteousness, things within that do not align with God's truth come up to be healed. Even in our darkest, most terrifying moments, we can have faith deep down that by the grace of God, all is well. Very soon, persecutions give way to spiritual understanding, and then we gain a peace like we have never known. We can choose loving thoughts and be gentle with ourselves as we ride the waves of uncertainty, growth, and change. Let us remember our freedom of thought and the power of faith and use these gifts wisely to attain peace under all circumstances.

In Jesus's name, amen.

Daily reading: Matthew 21:22 and Matthew 5:10–12

You were taught, regarding your former way of life, to put off your old self, which is being corrupted by its deceitful desires; to be made new. (Ephesians 4:22–23 NIV)

DAY 30

Affirmation

I live in spirit by allowing God's love to guide me.

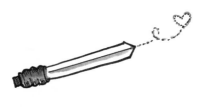

In stillness, I no longer squirm,
Uncomfortable in my own skin.
Years of keeping busy,
Distracting my mind,
Running, running, running
Until I could run no more.
And in that moment of collapse, I found relief.
Silently I gave over my free will,
And God filled my being with light.
Holy Spirit now guides my every step,
Slow and steady, healing
With the will of God,
Paving my way.

Meditation

Let us stop sleepwalking around, avoiding the needed healing process so long overdue! May we all give in to living in spirit and truth and lay everything at the feet of God, who loves us like no other ever could. The gift of free will is useless if we do not know how to use it for the greater good. When we give over our free will to God, we ask him to show us what to do, allowing us time to heal from the traumas of our lives. We have lived backward for so long, putting body ahead of spirit and causing so much suffering to ourselves. We were intended to live with the body in submission to the spirit, not the other way around. So many of us have been taught that we must stop sinning to have good lives, yet sinning is but a symptom of believing lies that are destructive to us. Once we wake up to God's truth and realize that we are not sinners but rather beings of God who have been tricked into thinking we are bad or faulty, it is then that sinning falls away because it is no longer needed to cope. We need deliverance from all the lies hidden in our minds so we can live in spirit and truth. Angels are all around to help us, if only we ask God for his perfect will to unfold. Let us begin receiving the gifts we were meant to have by turning our lives over to our all-knowing, all-loving God, who is waiting for us to open our hearts and ask for help.

In Jesus's name, amen.
Daily reading: 1 Corinthians 14:11–22 and 1 Timothy 4:14–16

DAY 31

Affirmation

By the grace of God, all is well.

When you lay down your life
Through prayer with faith,
Rest assured that even in hardship,
Holy Spirit is working on your behalf.
By the grace of God, all is well.

Meditation

Let us take great comfort in knowing that when we invite God to take over our lives, all things begin to work for our highest good. Miracles will become a common occurrence in our lives. Our only job is to be loving in all we do and have faith that God, as the force of love, is taking care of everything. Our perception will begin to shift as our minds restore to the original, divine blueprint they were meant to be. We can help this shift along by focusing our attention on the good that is manifesting in our lives. It can take us time to change our thinking patterns to see the love in everything even through the chaos. We can do the work of practicing pulling our thoughts back in the direction of love as we allow God to handle the rest for us. As we share everything that is on our hearts with the loving Creator, we are filled with comfort and love. God shows us the answers to all we ask of him in his perfect time and gives us spiritual understanding. God knows just when we are ready to handle more knowledge. Asking for God's will to be done in all aspects of our lives ensures the best outcomes. Let us nurture this intimate relationship and trust in the love and grace we can count on from God.

In Jesus's name, amen.
Daily reading: John 14:12 and Mark 16:20

DAY 32

Affirmation

We are all one in unity through God's love.

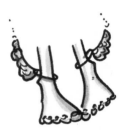

Source, God, Creator, Higher Power, Lord, Father, Yahweh.
With many walks of life,
There are many different names.
Yet all can agree on one thing:
This intelligent and divine force
Operates through the power of love.

Meditation

Let us not get caught up in the terminology and different labels used to name the one Creator, God. We have so much information coming at us and so many different beliefs that it becomes confusing. We all seek truth, and it can be overwhelming when there is conflicting information everywhere we look. Yet there is a way to know whether something is truth. When we hear something that is true, it will resonate with our hearts and feel right. It may even feel somehow familiar, like something we already knew somewhere within us. The foundation of every truth is always love—always! If a belief is fear based, it is not truth. This is true in every culture or faith. Even though we may use a different name for God than another, we can still honor others and realize that ultimately, we are all one people connected through God's love. Let us all find truth by listening with our hearts and not getting caught up in terminology. Our command from God is to love one another without judgment or condition. Jesus makes clear that we do not battle flesh and blood. He also stresses the importance of brotherly love and unity. As we put down any bias or assumption we may have about others, we are free to love, forgive, and enjoy our differences. May we all rise into the kingdom of God by seeing each other through eyes of pure love.

In Jesus's name, amen.
Daily reading: Exodus 3:14 and Revelation 22:13

DAY 33

Affirmation

I stand still, knowing God is in control.

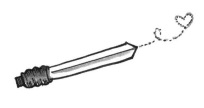

In the eye of the storm, be still.
The view from here is a bit scary,
Yet all is calm and safe.
Breathe and observe
Majestic, raging beauty,
Divine chaos that will bring forth growth
In ways we cannot even comprehend.

Meditation

Let us take heart that just like the Earth and the universe, our lives also have necessary storms. When we practice and seek to always be a loving force in every aspect of our lives, we will remain safely in the eye of every storm. Often things that feel like disruptions, defeats, or blockages are the Holy Spirit working to help us grow and move our lives in the right direction. Even outbursts in our relationship can be needed to clear away old patterns and move into healthier bonds. The sword of the Holy Spirit cuts away the things that go against our true nature and hold us back from our full potential. We can breathe a sigh of relief knowing the spirit of God's love always works for the good in our lives. This force is intelligent beyond our comprehension and is set into motion by our intention to be loving people. We will make mistakes and repeatedly must bring our focus back to love, but rest assured Holy Spirit is there to help. If God is our foundation, we will remain grounded in love. Let us remain calm knowing that perfect love heals all things.

In Jesus's name, amen.
Daily reading: 2 Timothy 2:19 and Matthew 7:24

DAY 34

Affirmation

I now allow God to heal all generational trauma and miscreation's.

The power of a story, like the waves of waters deep,
Sends my spirits rising, like a ship pushed out to sea,
Flowing smooth through verses, rough against the tide.
This story swims within my veins, a wild and stormy ride.

Meditation

Let us realize the importance of our ancestral story. Our DNA carries the cellular memory of all the generations before us—the blessings as well as the so-called curses. As we observe how our thoughts, will, and emotions manifest out into our physical reality, we can begin to see all the manifestations we did not consciously intend—the miscreation's. We are working toward creating the life we desire now by consciously manifesting with righteousness, loving thought, and intention. As we work toward this mastery, let us remember that we are helping future generations. Our cells hold the memory and create the new blueprint for offspring. With this in mind, we can call forth deliverance, healing, and reimprinting of all the miscreation's we have inherited through our family line. God will guide us through this process with his Holy Spirit. Every life tells a unique story of its own that can teach us so many things. Taking the time to write our own stories is a powerful tool to help us on our healing journeys. Writing our stories empowers us as we release our emotions on paper and sort out parts of our lives that may have been confusing to us before. Even researching family history can help us uncover clues to our inherited DNA blueprint. This offers us the opportunity to heal our entire bloodline. Let us begin to honor the importance of our stories and the power held within our DNA.

In Jesus's name, amen.
Daily reading: Numbers 14:18 and Exodus 34:7

DAY 35

Affirmation

I wait on the will of heaven with patience and faith.

Desperate for a solution, I move in haste,
Deceived about the intention of my will.
The problem dies, but new ones take its place.
My impulses leave me with deep regret.

Meditation

Let us take time to collect ourselves. So many of us may be tempted to act on impulses when we are in transitions or painful times of our lives. Healing and restoration are processes that take time, and many of us want to rush through them too quickly. Maybe we are in situations that are not serving our best interests. We can gently remind ourselves that we do not need to act in haste to make changes in our lives. Jesus, in his famous Sermon on the Mount, declared, "Blessed are the peacemakers, for they shall be called children of God" (Matthew 5:9 NIV). Peacemakers are those who use prayer to apply God's love as the healing salve to all problems. In prayer, we return to the presence of God and commune with him. This is the secret place where our characters and souls are changed, and only then can the outer change for any good. Prayer is contemplation in the presence of God. This silent work gives God the power to heal and transform us. This is the path to serenity. One who has serenity can be a peacemaker. Let us take all the time we need to be still and collect our true selves before making major decisions. It is better to wait on the will of heaven than to push our own will. Let us be still, trusting that inner growth continues even in our stillness because God is orchestrating all we need.

In Jesus's name, amen.
Daily reading: Proverbs 3:5–6

DAY 36

Affirmation

I bring into my awareness the blessings of this moment.

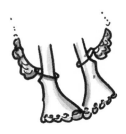

I will not crave for things
Or wish for better times.
I will trust that where I am today
Has been planned by the one Divine.

Meditation

Let us remember that suffering comes when we crave things we do not have or wish our lives were different than they are. When we let go of our desire for things we do not have, we let go of our suffering as well. This is not to say we do not strive for a better life; it simply means we accept where we are. As we call forth God's divine guidance, we can breathe into the peace and love by which we are surrounded. God's love is always there engulfing us, yet we need to bring it into our awareness. The more often we pull our minds back into communion with God, the more we can see the blessings coming our way. We can have peace right now when we begin to realize that contentment is based on our gratefulness for what we do have. May we let go of cravings and see the goodness in our lives and the beauty of Holy Spirit working on our behalf.

In Jesus's name, amen.
Daily reading: John 4:14 and Hebrews 13:5

DAY 37

Affirmation

I release all that no longer serves my highest good.

I board this little raft of hope
with the Captain of the sea,
sinking ship left behind,
my dreams in front of me.

Meditation

Let us remember that through our healing journey, we are never alone. Many of us have abandoned parts of our lives that are not serving our highest good. This can seem scary for us to leave behind the life with which we have become familiar. Still, sometimes our old ways of living must be abandoned like a sinking ship. Often, when we resist these changes, the Holy Spirit steps in and forces us in ways that feel like a crisis, yet our highest good is always being sought for us. Divine intervention can be masked in the most turbulent of times. It may be a long journey to calm waters, but we can trust in God's love to guide us all the way. May we relax and enjoy the ride, knowing we are in good hands.

In Jesus's name, amen.
Daily reading: Psalm 23:1–6

DAY 38

Affirmation

I now live in spirit and truth.

Like a transplanted tree,
I sever my roots from the dictates of my past.
For a short time, I wither in shock.
Then I begin to flourish
as my roots deepen
in my new rich soil.

Meditation

Let us affirm our right to choose a life filled with love and joy. Did we grow up receiving the love we needed and deserved? Were we raised with the carnal mind being the focus, conforming us to the world around us? Now, as God transforms us to be spiritually minded, we see that we must make some changes in who we spend our time with. The spiritually minded will be seekers of truth, love, and service to others over themselves. When we live this way, we are in the flow of God's love, and all things we need are cared for. The carnal minds will be seekers of selfish desires that only temporarily serve them. They do not have access to the law of God's love to adjust and correct all errors in their lives, as the spiritual-minded ones do. When we strive to live in spirit, our blessings are so powerful and constant. God will manifest our needs and desires so fast that we will not even have time to stress about where things will come from. The Holy Spirit finds miraculous ways of making all things work for the good for those who live in love and truth. The spiritual mind knows "Ask God, believe, receive, and be grateful" as the simple formula for manifesting all our loving desires.

In Jesus's name, amen.
Daily reading: John 4:24 and John 15:7

DAY 39

Affirmation

I will act only when my intention is loving.

May all action flow from our hearts
So that innocence can be restored to the world.

Meditation

Let us always strive to act with loving intentions, for therein lies innocence and grace. When we live from this place, we are being our God-given, authentic selves, the people God created us to be. Deep within our hearts, God has embedded our unique, divine plan. As our hearts are purified, this plan begins to unfold. We can help along this process by lifting ourselves from the ebb and flow of life to check our intentions and make sure they are not distorted with any malicious intent. As we heal and begin to see the truth of our intentions, we can do the inner work needed to release the programming of revenge and paying back hurts. That old programming has never served our good; it kept us in a dualistic mindset of separation. We are now developing a unity mindset of love and oneness. As we pause and bring our focus back to God, we can find our deepest truth and act from this place of love. Let us keep aligning ourselves daily with God's peace and love so we can act from this beautiful state of being.

In Jesus's name, amen.
Daily reading: John 13:34–35 and Proverbs 17:20

DAY 40

Affirmation

*I will be still and allow my grief to be felt,
processed, and released in a healthy way.*

Running in circles,
Discomfort everywhere I go.
Feeling so displaced,
Where I want to feel at home.

Meditation

Let us remember that wherever we go, there we are. We cannot run from our emotions; they will follow with us. Many of us struggle so much with feelings that we run from place to place, hoping something will make us feel better. Emotions are energy in motion and need to be felt, processed, and released to be well. Emotions that we do not allow ourselves to feel, process, and release cause the energy to be trapped within our bodies, where it eventually condenses into matter. That is how disease is formed. Different types of unreleased emotion turn into certain diseases, such as the unhealed pain of heartache and betrayal, where unforgiveness and resentment can become malignant within our cells. The only way to find peace is to stop and take the time to find the true source of the emotion with which we are struggling. When little things that happen in life irritate us, and we begin to blame others for what we are going through, that is a sign we are not dealing with a deeper issue within. Instead of trying to find outside distractions to blame or even make us feel better, we can uncover what we are truly feeling within. From there, we can act. Could it be that we have stifled grief from some sort of loss that we never allowed ourselves to grieve over? The only cure for grieving is to grieve. Jesus said in Matthew 5:4 (NIV), "Blessed are those who mourn, for they will be comforted." The comfort comes as we release the emotions. We must mourn when we need to to be emotionally healthy. Let us honor our feelings by looking for the true source rather than trying to brush them away.

In Jesus's name, amen.
Daily reading: Psalm 34:18

DAY 41

Affirmation

My faith is moving mountains.

I wish and dream with strong intent
Of the life I know my soul was meant;
Joy and peace this life will bring.
My heart will dance; my soul will sing.
Before my eyes, it all will be
This life my mind already sees.

Meditation

Let us hold loving intentions of the life we desire. What do we really wish to be doing with our lives? What is our souls' true purpose? Clues are found in the things that bring us joy and passion. If money and income were no issue and we had all we needed financially, what would we choose as our lives' work? What brings us joy and makes our hearts sing? Let us visualize our dreams with such love and intensity that all obstacles begin to melt away. We are cocreators with God. We have the power to manifest anything we can dream of that is in line with God's will. With love and faith in God, there are no impossibilities. Our thoughts, intentions, visions, and words are tools we can use to bring forth our hearts' desires. When our desires have loving, pure intent, we have the backing of God. First John 4:12 (ESV) says, "If we love one another, God abides in us and his love is perfected in us." Doors we never imagined will begin to open for us as we abide in God. We can walk through them with peace and faith that our desires will surely come to fruition.

In Jesus's name, amen.
Daily reading: James 2:26 and 1 Corinthian 13:2

DAY 42

Affirmation

In stillness, I breathe my way into the realm of spirit.

Waves of love wash through me
As I let go of the physical,
Embracing the silence.
Consciously and quietly I float,
Feeling my spirit blend into all that is.

Meditation

Let us remember that just beyond the realm of the physical, our spirits bear witness with God, and we connect with all of humanity through powerful waves of God's love. We can consciously begin to feel this connection through meditation. As we allow ourselves to let go of our body awareness a little more with each breath, we can allow our minds to quiet. Soon we begin to feel a calm washing through us. This is the love of God that connects us all. In this meditative state, there is nothing to do but be and absorb the power of God's love into our every fiber. This power restores us. It can melt away any blocked emotion and fill those spaces with the light of God's love. Once we invite this in, we simply need to breathe and allow it to flow through us. May we make the time each day to soak in the Holy Spirit and rest in this place of healing love.

In Jesus's name, amen.
Daily reading: Zephaniah 3:17 and 1 John 4:16

DAY 43

Affirmation

I use my words to lift people up.

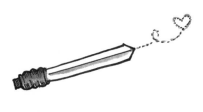

An honorable man holds his tongue when angry.
He knows his words can cut deep into the hearts
of those he loves, hurting their spirits,
while his songs of praise make their spirits soar.

Meditation

Let us practice expressing our emotions softly. We can take time to be silent and plan out how we will express our feelings. Many of us have said hurtful things when we were hurt or angry. This damages not only those we are directing our anger at but also ourselves. Galatians 6:7 (NIV) states, "A man reaps what he sows." This goes both for good and bad. We are not speaking truth when we are being hurtful. In Matthew 15:11 (NIV), Jesus says, "What goes into someone's mouth does not defile them, but what comes out of their mouth, that is what defiles them." We must be careful with not only what we say but also what we think, because right thinking will produce right action. Taking a step back and seeking the guidance of God or trusted friends can be useful to process emotions before acting. Let us protect ourselves and those we love by practicing healthy ways to express our feelings.

In Jesus's name, amen.
Daily reading: Matthew 15:11 and Mark 7:15

DAY 44

Affirmation

I stand firm on a foundation of God's love.

One tiny, loose stone
Swept out of its resting place
In the turbulent rain
Begins the avalanche.

Meditation

Let us do our best to stay on emotionally stable ground by caring for our needs. When we get overwhelmed and snared into destructive behavior, it impacts all those close to us—and those close to them as well. An avalanche of chaos can ensue. People love and care for us, which feeds and nurtures our souls. It also means that we give back to create an even exchange of giving and receiving. We all go through tough times and need uplifting; this is a natural part of life. Yet we must be careful to find healthy ways to cope with stress. When we turn to methods of blocking out or self-medicating, we can end up making things worse. We owe it to ourselves and those who count on us to be responsible for our mental and emotional health. By focusing on loving ourselves the way God loves us, we can make sure we are doing our best to be on a healing path rather than a destructive one.

In Jesus's name, amen.
Daily reading: Ecclesiastes 3:1–22

DAY 45

Affirmation

I am shifting beyond my carnal mind and into my spiritual mind.

I open my mind to the pain of others,
Cradling humanity in my heart.
Judgments dissolve from my mind
As I breathe into love.

Meditation

Let us remember that people are not their behaviors. Even when we do not like or approve of someone's behavior, we can still have love for them. Jesus came here to teach us unconditional love and the mighty power that love carries. He taught us that it is not our God-given, true nature when we act in ways that do not align with love. We can easily rebuke any false belief that is not of God by remembering who we truly are. We all are working on shaking off the conditioning we grew up in and the ego programming of the world. When judgments come to the surface or upset gets triggered in us, it is showing us where old programming is still in place. We all mirror each other, and clues of what needs healing within ourselves are often seen in what we struggle with in others. It can be difficult to stay in a place of love when we wrongly judge others. We do not know all the dynamics of others' lives and all the variables involved in their choices. We do not know the depths of their pain, struggles, traumas, upbringing, or mental health. Therefore, we cannot correctly judge based on behaviors we see. We must open our spiritual eyes and look beyond the surface. The only way to do this is through the eyes of love. Just as we can still unconditionally love our parents and our children despite all their mistakes, we can offer this kind of love and compassion to all of humanity. As we allow ourselves to see where we are still holding on to the mindsets of the lower carnal mind, we can begin to shift into the higher state of consciousness of the spiritual mind, where only love and truth is seen.

In Jesus's name, amen.
Daily reading: 1 Peter 3:18 and Galatians 5:16

DAY 46

Affirmation

I take timely retreats to replenish my soul.

Curled up tight, my body trembles.
Depleted and weak, I retreat.
Alone with the angels, I rest
As my soul is restored.

Meditation

Let us notice the physical signs of our energy being depleted. Many of us will have times that we give and give to others to the point of draining the vital life energy we need to sustain ourselves. There are times when we have no choice but to keep on giving, such as taking care of a loved one whose life depends on us or during a tragedy. We are instilled with survival mechanisms to get us through those times. We may find ourselves on autopilot for prolonged periods. At some point, though, we must trust our physical bodies to let us know when it is time to step back from giving and fill up ourselves. We can sustain survival mode for only so long before we crash. Feeling exhausted, sore, achy, irritable, and sick are signs that we are giving away too much of our energy. Those are the times we must turn to God to find reprieve. Asking for what we need through prayer is vital if we are to maintain. When we are so depleted that we do not even know what we need anymore, let us take great comfort that the Creator does know. We can put it all in the hands of God and allow ourselves to let go and recover with faith that we will be cared for perfectly. Let us seek balance and wellness for ourselves first and foremost so we have the energy to give to others.

In Jesus's name, amen.
Daily reading: Philippians 4:13 and 1 Peter 5:10

DAY 47

Affirmation

I nurture my spirit through joy.

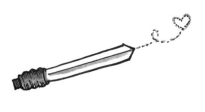

The catcher of my dreams,
The keeper of my song.
My spirit is my dearest friend
That guides me to where I belong.

Meditation

Let us remember to nurture our spirits. We may not always feel as if we know ourselves very well, but we can trust that God knows us on a deep spiritual level. Our spirits are who we truly are, and they are our connection to God. Nurturing our spirits involves doing things that bring us joy, wonder, and love. We must remember that it is possible to have joy and sorrow simultaneously. When we are in sorrow, let us take time out to balance it with joy. Creativity, meditating, learning, or simply being in nature all feeds our spirits. Just as we need to care for our physical bodies daily, our spirits need daily care as well. Let us seek the joy, love, and wonder we need to be well.

In Jesus's name, amen.
Daily reading: Psalm 16:11 and Psalm 23:1–6

DAY 48

Affirmation

I love myself as God does.

Wisdom to know I deserve goodness.
Discernment to set boundaries of protection.
Imagination to visualize my dreams.
Power of intention to bring them to life.
Knowing the wisdom my heart holds.
These are the gifts that come with self-love.

Meditation

Let us know the importance of loving ourselves. All the qualities required for attaining the life we desire stem from self-love. When we know we are deserving of the life we desire and tell ourselves that, we open ourselves to wisdom. We begin to believe we are deserving of achieving our dreams. This knowing helps us develop our intuition and gives us discernment of people and situations that either support or hinder our highest good. We can then set healthy boundaries to protect ourselves. These wonderful qualities work together to help us manifest our dreams. It all begins with seeing ourselves through the eyes of God and loving who we are. God intimately created us with a purpose in mind. We are made in God's very image and are therefore a reflection of God. Jesus spoke of the importance of loving God and others, and that includes ourselves. From that love, all else falls into place with ease. Let us access the gifts that come from self-love as we realize more and more how lovable we truly are.

In Jesus's name, amen.
Daily reading: Psalm 139:13–16 and Genesis 1:27

DAY 49

Affirmation

Solutions come with ease as I rise into spirit.

I shall focus with strong intent,
Looking right past my problems
To harmonious solutions.
I will be blind to blame
And deaf to judgments,
Ridding myself of all difficulty.

Meditation

Let us strive for peace and harmony in all our affairs. It can be hard to look past the drama of a difficult situation, especially for those of us who have become accustomed to chaos in our lives. As we focus on rising into living in spirit, truth, and love, we bring into our awareness the support of God that surrounds us. That support is there to assist us if we only ask. God is working through us always, and as we bring that into our conscious minds, our perspective shifts into our loving, true nature. This is where we connect with God and find our peaceful solutions. All can be reconciled when we seek the force of God's Holy Spirit to bring harmony. When we are tempted to pass blame or judgment, we can gently bring our minds back to loving resolutions. Those around us may not do the same and still we can remain true to our hearts and values. This will bring peace to our lives. Let us not seek to avoid problems rather strive to handle them with love.

In Jesus's name, amen.
Daily reading: Philippians 4:6–13

DAY 50

Affirmation

I embrace my ever-changing reality.

Refusing to make changes to my life,
Knowing my needs have changed,
Keeps me stuck in denial of reality
Rather than growing with new opportunities.

Meditation

Let us fully embrace life and flow with the changes we encounter. Sometimes our needs change, and we must adapt a new routine to maintain or establish wellness. We may find ourselves avoiding the need to end a relationship that has become unhealthy or to resist ending an unhealthy situation. Instead of fighting what life brings us, we can allow ourselves a period of grieving but then accept and adapt. We must remember that our peace comes from within. The spirit of God resides within us so we can have faith that our lives are in safe hands. We are given all the tools we need for anything life brings us. The people we need to support us always show up in our lives at the right time. The Holy Spirit is always ahead of us, paving the way and organizing the details. We must choose the path of love, and all will be well. Let us lean on each other through difficult changes and face our challenges with open hearts and minds.

In Jesus's name, amen.
Daily reading: 1 Corinthians 10:13

DAY 51

Affirmation

I am in but not of the world.

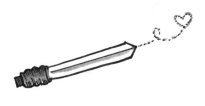

Wash away our judgments, remind us who we are:
Beautiful, tender spirits in a world that's all too hard.
A world that's filled with hardship weighing on our souls.
A world where many suffer and have no place to go.
A world that tells us lies and tricks us into greed,
That turns us on each other when love is all we need.

Meditation

Let us remember to step back from things in the world that hinder love, peace, and unity. The world is full of things that offer us ways to improve our well-being. We can now connect to others in amazing ways, and technology allows people opportunities they would never have had access to before now. On the flip side, the world also tempts us with greed, lust, and power, making these things seems okay and normal. Allowing ourselves to support and partake in things that hurt others and ourselves will dampen our spirits and push us away from who we truly are. We cannot have true happiness and joy when we are not being our authentic selves. God calls us to stand out from the world by being true to who we were created to be. Let us use our God-given sense of intuitive discernment to decide what does not belong in our lives.

In Jesus's name, amen.
Daily reading: Romans 12:2 and 1 John 4:4

DAY 52

Affirmation

I go easy on myself as I acclimate to a new way of living.

I will rest in this unfamiliar place
Until it becomes familiar.

Meditation

Let us remember that when we begin to live with love for ourselves, feelings of uneasiness may come over us. Things can feel unfamiliar and awkward at first. We may feel very alone as we develop new ways of living. We can remind ourselves that during this phase, it is normal to feel a bit disoriented. If we are not used to making choices for our own best interests, we may feel selfish at first. Putting ourselves first is not selfish at all; it is the most loving gift we can offer to others. When we are truly well, we have so much more to give. Taking time to sit quietly and breathe into the love from God that engulfs us always can calm these feelings. Let us remember that as we develop deeper love for ourselves, peace and joy will surely be ours.

In Jesus's name, amen.
Daily reading: 2 Corinthians 5:17 and 1 Corinthians 6:19–20

DAY 53

Affirmation

I rise above the judgments of others and stand firm in God's truth.

I will hold my head high
Among those who look down on me.
I will smile at their dirty looks.
I will sing praises for them when they curse me.
For I choose to live in love,
Even among those who still live in fear.

Meditation

Let us not be brought down by those who still operate from the false ego. Many of us have even had to break away from family members who are stuck in unhealthy patterns. Not reacting to those who oppose us is essential. We waste precious energy engaging in conflict. Even when someone has a negative perspective about us or says things that are untrue, we do not need to take on that person's judgments. It can be difficult to not get in our heads about what others think and say. Our best defense is to separate ourselves from those who do not have the ability to understand the changes we are making in our lives. Many are not yet spiritually awake and cannot comprehend anything beyond the things they see with their eyes. We can lovingly detach from these people. We can seek out new relationships with people who love God and support our growth in a positive way. Let us establish healthy boundaries to protect ourselves from those who drain our energy.

In Jesus's name, amen.
Daily reading: 2 Corinthians 6:14 and Romans 16:17

DAY 54

Affirmation

I now release and clear all sexual trauma from my body and my soul.

Flowing down the stream,
I am weightless,
One with the healing waters
That knows just where to go.

Meditation

Let us flow with the current of life with faith in God. As we abide in God, our lives will find a way of taking us exactly where we need to be and when we need to be there. When it is time to release old traumas from our being, experiences or situations will bring it up to the surface for healing. Many of us have had sexual trauma in our lives. Even the stigmas, shameful beliefs, and taboos about sexuality traumatize us. When they are not in line with truth and love, these beliefs hold us back from our full potential. When these things come up to be released, it can be extremely uncomfortable. We may find ourselves in a confusing internal battle. We can trust the Holy Spirit to bring all we need to find truth and resolution if we go within and ask God to guide us. Our lives will then guide us to the tools and ideas needed to release the old programming. Making sure we are grounded deep into God's love will help us go through these healings with more ease. Let us have faith in ourselves and in God to flow through our journey perfectly.

In Jesus's name, amen.
Daily reading: Psalm 34:4–5 and Psalm 3:3

DAY 55

Affirmation

I am remembering who I truly am.

Peeling back layers of grief
And all the traits acquired for survival,
Exposing this sweet, innocent child
Longing only to love.
I will be her mother.
I will nurture her with love and praise,
Like every child deserves.

Meditation

Let us go back and remember a place in time before we knew troubles or hurt, back when we were a young child. What if we were raised with perfect love? Never being yelled at, but rather being spoken to with gentle guidance, praise, and appreciation. Being encouraged to do the things we enjoyed and to believe in our dreams. Being taught with a gentle voice and never shamed. Only surrounded by loving people who lived in peace. Who would we be now if we were raised with perfect love? We would be our authentic selves. We may not have had this perfect childhood, but we can acknowledge that we indeed deserve it. We are children of the Most High. All that has been created by God is also loved by God perfectly. Let us offer ourselves that perfect love now and blossom into who we truly are.

In Jesus's name, amen.
Daily reading: Ephesians 3:17–19

DAY 56

Affirmation

My well-being comes from within.

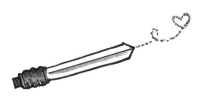

This bee came out of nowhere,
And disturb him I did not.
Yet still he came and stung me.
The sting was quick and hot;
It burned for several moments.
Then I went about my day.
No bee will ever bring me down
Or steal my joy away!

Meditation

Let us remember that we are responsible for how we let things impact us. When we have been practicing loving and accepting ourselves, this comes much easier. In the past, certain comments may have hurt us and disturbed our well-being. Yet like the bee sting, we have a choice to not take it personal. We can now recognize that it is never the comment that damages us; it is what we do with it in our minds. We have a choice to hang on to things and dwell on them, or to shake them off. Some hurtful experiences may need to be addressed, but they never need to define or damage our self-worth. When we are wronged or someone acts in an unloving way toward us, we must bring the matter to God in prayer as soon as possible. The sooner we can forgive the person, the safer we are from resentment taking hold of us. When we forgive and release people from our judgment, we are turning it over to God to handle. God can then move in amazing ways to reconcile or remove these difficulties from our life. It is God who must handle these matters and direct us in what our part is. We can always handle these types of situations with love by going in prayer. We have complete control over this. Let us remember our ability to be well even under difficult circumstances. God will use everything for the good when we turn it over in prayer.

In Jesus's name, amen.
Daily reading: Psalm 73:26 and Isaiah 41:10

DAY 57

Affirmation

I have dominion over my life.

My spirit remembers my purpose.
My heart guides the way.
My mind sends out affirming thought waves.
My life then responds to my requests.

Meditation

Let us honor our whole selves. We are not just bodies; we are much more complex than that. We have spirits that are all knowing and connect us to all that is. Our spirits reside within us but also extend far beyond us and carry the memory of our purpose. When we align our hearts with God through prayer and meditation, we connect ourselves to God's will. As we begin to know and trust God's voice in our hearts, our minds can align with this. When our thoughts are loving and positive, they create a positive emotional response in us as well; these emotions carry power that help us move closer to our dreams. As we align our minds, will, and emotions with God's divine love, we create the life we desire. We must practice being mindful of the thoughts we have. If our minds are predominantly full of thoughts of doom and gloom and all the things we do not like, that is what we are going to create in our lives. When our minds are focused on love, compassion, and peace, we create more of that into our lives. Let us tap into our ability to fulfill our dreams by practicing sending positive and loving thoughts out into the world around us.

In Jesus's name, amen.
Daily reading: Proverbs 4:23 and 2 Corinthians 10:3–5

DAY 58

Affirmation

I rest in faith of God's divine timing.

I awoke,
I remembered,
and finally everything made sense.

Meditation

Let us trust that there is a rhyme and reason for life that is still just beyond our comprehension. We can trust that we are being guided and protected perfectly. When we are living in truth and love, God's spiritual guidance is available to us. We do not need to define or even understand this amazing force to acknowledge it is real and powerful. We soon will gain more awareness as we release more and more of the old programs and conditioning our minds have learned. As we awake to truth, things become clearer. Just as we can trust the lights to go on when we flip the switch, we can trust that guidance and comfort will be there when we ask for God's divine help. As we go through the process of spiritual awakening, let us trust the knowing of our hearts and have faith that we are never alone.

In Jesus's name, amen.
Daily reading: Jeremiah 29:11–14

DAY 59

Affirmation

I am in the fullness of God's love.

Once only fleeting glimpses of joy, wonder, and peace
Now become my natural state of being
More and more each passing day.

Meditation

As we shed old beliefs, patterns, mindsets, and limitations, let us be filled with excitement for the life that God is creating for us. In this new life we are building with God, we get to decided what belongs and what does not serve us well by tuning in to what God is showing us. We can continue removing obstacles as we develop deeper love for God, ourselves, and others in a way we never have before. Unconditional love will carry us beyond our prior limits. With the power of God's love as the driving force in our lives, we are open to endless possibilities. Let us rejoice in this truth.

In Jesus's name, amen.
Daily reading: Mark 9:23 and Matthew 21:21

DAY 60

Affirmation

This too shall pass.

The dust will settle,
as too will these emotions.
Time and gentleness will move this along.

Meditation

Let us remember that emotions come and go. When we are dealing with painful emotions, it can feel dark and scary. The urge to escape uncomfortable feelings can be strong. We can rest in knowing that feelings never last forever; they are ever changing. We can help ourselves handle our difficult feelings by acknowledging them and talking them through. We can remember that emotions are energy in motion that we do not want to build up in us; rather, they should pass through us. Maybe we are dealing with feelings of remorse. When we know we have hurt another, it is natural to have regrets. We can be with our feelings without collapsing ourselves in them or forming judgments because of them. As we seek to know God's will in all situations, we can have faith that we will be shown the steps to resolve and move past difficult feelings. Let us be gentle with ourselves as we work through our emotions.

In Jesus's name, amen.
Daily reading: Ecclesiastes 3:4 and John 11:35

DAY 61

Affirmation

I now ask the Holy Spirit to transform all shame into truth.

Before I knew your lies were lies,
I trusted you.
And I was ashamed of myself
Because you said I should be.
And I cried in silence
So you didn't see
That I was only feeling sorry for myself again.

Meditation

Let us reject all the old lies we were raised to believe. Anything that produced feelings of shame was indeed a lie! Many of us have gone through life denying ourselves of compassion and love because of old programming. We no longer need to live this way. God made us to be vessels of divine love. The people in our life have unconsciously engaged in breaking the spirit of love that we are. We can acknowledge that it was wrong even if it was our own parents who unknowingly shamed us. We do not need to carry anger toward them; they surely did not know the impact of their harsh words and teachings. Yet we must reprogram from destructive thought patterns that were put in place. Let us recognize these old patterns as they arise and replace them with love and truth. God is helping us to use these experiences to help others, and this is how we can transform it all to love. May we lift ourselves and others into the truth of the love that we are.

In Jesus's name, amen.
Daily reading: 1 John 4:16

DAY 62

Affirmation

I now remove all filters and see the beauty of every being.

Intricate beauty runs deep within us all.
Awestruck those will be who catch just a glimpse.
But only eyes of love can see beyond the surface.
Blessed are the few whose vision remains pure.

Meditation

Let us strive to see everything with eyes of God. Like a baby looking at its mother, only beauty is seen. Even pain has a certain beauty. When we focus our attention on what really matters, we can begin to see everything in a loving light. We do not need to judge anyone when we possess the knowledge that under the surface, all beings have a pure beautiful spirit, including ourselves. Outer appearances may tell a story of where we have been but never about who we are. Let us focus our vision and see with new loving eyes the spirit of love all around us.

In Jesus's name, amen.
Daily reading: 1 Peter 3:3–4

DAY 63

Affirmation

I accept responsibility for my actions without blaming others.

When I woke to your sad eyes,
my heart went still
to know I hurt you so.
This somberness I cannot shake.

Meditation

Let us remember that we all hurt the ones we love at times. Taking responsibility for our wrongs can be so difficult. Many times, our first instinct is to justify our behavior by making excuses, yet that never serves any good. Making things right is usually as simple as acknowledging our wrong and offering compassion. Love forgives simply because we are loved, yet trust is something we must work at. When others are hurt, offering them validation and compassion will build deeper trust. The Holy Spirit can reconcile all things when we humble ourselves and are honest about our mistakes. May we find the courage to take responsibility for all our actions, especially when they have impacted others.

In Jesus's name, amen.
Daily reading: Matthew 5:23–24

DAY 64

Affirmation

I live in spirit on the earthly plane.

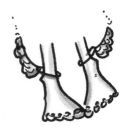

This ordinary life of mine
In the midst of this confusing world.
I will live it in a nonordinary way,
Being in but not of this world.

Meditation

Let us always walk to the beat of God's loving heart. Even when the majority does not, let us be firm in our will to live lives of love. We are true to our nature when we live modest lives where we do not give ourselves airs; rather, we do our tasks for the task's sake. We find our joy in using our special, God-given gifts and passions as we continue getting to know who we truly are at the core and adapt our lives accordingly. Being our true selves aligns us with God and will bring us peace. Let us be who we are even amid adversity.

In Jesus's name, amen.
Daily reading: Matthew 5:14 and 1 John 3:18

DAY 65

Affirmation

I will to do God's will.

As I surrender my will for God's,
I become closer to my own true will,
The will I have forgotten.
For I have gained another set of eyes,
Eyes that remember and see all,
A master guide to lead me.

Meditation

Let us remember that surrendering our will to God is not giving up our hopes and dreams. Our purpose and our true will for ourselves is one in the same with God's will for us. When we surrender our will, we are simply opening ourselves up to divine guidance to help lead us in the best possible way to our true purpose. The Holy Spirit is eager to join forces and help us, yet we must ask due to the laws of free will under which we live. We give nothing up by acknowledging our current human limits and trusting God's will to be perfect. God remembers our purpose here, even when we have forgotten. As we heal and grow, we begin to realize who we are and why we are here. We are wise to enlist the help of the Holy Spirit to take charge for us. Let us trust in God to lead us along.

In Jesus's name, amen.
Daily reading: Ephesians 5:17 and Psalm 119:105

DAY 66

Affirmation

May all I do be done with love.

Not sure what's right or wrong,
Not sure where to go,
Not sure what I believe in.
But there is one thing I know.
I know how to love,
And if that is all I do,
I guess I really can't go wrong
Since love is always true.

Meditation

Let us not waste time or energy worrying about what we should be doing with our lives. We all question our choices from time to time and wonder what if we had done things differently. Many of us are not even sure what we believe in anymore. Yet we are where we are, and that is a good starting point. We do not need to fret over our futures; we can let them unfold naturally. We have put God in the driver's seat of our lives, and we can trust that all will be revealed to us as we go. When we are living with love as our driving force, we can never go wrong. Let us live peacefully as we love passionately.

In Jesus's name, amen.
Daily reading: John 14:27 and Galatians 6:2

DAY 67

Affirmation

I am perfect just as I am.

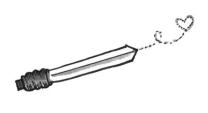

I will embrace every little piece of me—
My body, mind, and spirit.

Meditation

Let us see the true essence of our beauty. Many of us have been falsely told how we should look or act to be the perfect man or woman. We can embrace our bodies and our minds knowing we are wonderful exactly as we are. We are beautiful portals for God's love to bless this earthly plane. We all have our own unique qualities that make us special. We can celebrate these qualities by doing special things to care for ourselves. Treating ourselves daily in some small way can help boost our sense of worth, whether it is putting on lotion, indulging in a bubble bath, stretching, reading a good book, praying, or simply meditating. Let us embrace our beautiful individuality each day.

In Jesus's name, amen.
Daily reading: 1 Timothy 4:3–4

DAY 68

Affirmation

I do without doing, and still everything gets done.

To honor my spirit,
I must not go beyond my current limits.
I will go within and be receptive
To God's voice in my heart.

Meditation

Let us remember our limitations and not try to reach beyond what we are comfortably able to handle right now. We may feel a measure of progress in our healing and be tempted to take on more than we should. Let us continue being gentle on ourselves and slowly ease our way into the life God is creating for us. When we lift our lives up to God in prayer, things get done without effort on our part. It is God doing for us. Our main goal can be getting comfortable with being true to who we are in Christ before we take on the world. This way, as we begin doing more, we will have a more balanced way of handling life that promotes our well-being rather than draining us. We can practice being still and seeking the guidance of Holy Spirit before taking on new things. Let us be content as we slowly acclimate to living mindfully of God's presence.

In Jesus's name, amen.
Daily reading: Matthew 11:29

DAY 69

Affirmation

I now allow the deepest truth to come to the surface.

All these feelings raging through me,
Overwhelming my mind.
All the while, life continues coming at me.
Stepping back from it all for just a moment,
I begin to understand
Just what these feelings are.

Meditation

Let us take the time to be self-aware. We can begin by noticing our feelings and the physical reactions they bring. Sorting out why we react the way we do to things will come with time. The first step is recognizing where we are at. When we feel triggered, we can look to see whether there is a deeper, old program running in our minds that has not been released. We are seeking deliverance from any hidden lies within our minds. Stepping back from daily life to touch base with how we are feeling can help to heighten our awareness of what still needs healing within us. When we allow ourselves to observe without judgment how we are feeling, it gives us time to think and sort out our feelings before we decide how to react outwardly. Let us practice using our spiritual eyes and ears to see the deeper truths that may be hidden. Then we can mindfully ask God to remove these hindrances from us.

In Jesus's name, amen.
Daily reading: Jeremiah 5:21 and 2 Corinthians 4:18

DAY 70

Affirmation

As I observe life, I see that all is well.

As my mind gets cluttered
And life confuses me,
I can switch into observer mode,
Disconnecting my emotions,
Simply observing the happenings
With no feelings attached.
From this vantage point, I can see
That I am still just fine.

Meditation

Let us strive to keep a positive perspective despite all outside circumstances swirling around us. We must remember that no matter what is happening, we are okay. We can choose not to take on feelings of fear and uncertainty even when it appears that chaos surrounds us. The reality is that we can have peace even in times of trouble by simply changing our focus and leaning on God. During times in our lives when our emotions begin to overwhelm us, let us bring our hearts back to a place of love by disconnecting briefly. It may help to imagine we are observing the life of a friend. What would we see if it was not our own life? Then we can gently breathe in God's love and exhale that love on to all matters in our lives. Let us do what we must to keep our focus on the peace that comes from God's love.

In Jesus's name, amen.
Daily reading: Philippians 3:14 and 2 Thessalonians 3:16

DAY 71

Affirmation

With God's protection, I can allow myself full healing.

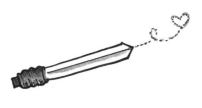

Trying to ignore this wound
And live as if it never happened.
But it keeps breaking open
Deeper than before.
Finally I have no choice—
I must stop everything.
Inspect, cleanse, cover, rest, repeat.
From the inside out, I slowly heal.

Meditation

Let us attend to our emotional wounds promptly, just as we would for a physical injury. We can notice the signs of emotional injury such as anxiety, fear, anger, sorrow, depression, and low self-worth. These symptoms indicate that an emotional wound has been left unattended. We can apply the same principles of healing a physical wound to our emotional wounds. Let us seek the guidance of the Holy Spirit to uncover what is hidden within us. We can call forth knowledge and then keep a keen spiritual eye open for the answers that come to us. May we take the time to nurture and heal from all that hinders our well-being.

In Jesus's name, amen.
Daily reading: Psalm 91:4–6 and Psalm 34:4

DAY 72

Affirmation

I stand unshaken on a foundation of God's love.

You tell me I would be perfect if only,
And you point out every flaw you see.
I simply reject your point of view
And go about my life, unaffected.
I have learned to do that these days.

Meditation

Let us not overanalyze or give any of our energy to criticism from others. We can know and love ourselves enough now to reject all negativity that comes our way. Our God-given authority over our lives enables us to keep a protective barrier from this. As we continue discovering the depth of our beauty that God has woven into our every fiber, we become grounded in God's protective love. We will never change others, but we can change the way we are impacted by them. When we firmly stand in God's righteousness, our hearts are shielded. Soon we get to a point where comments that used to hurt us hold no weight and are easily shaken off. We are now living in love and in the truth of spirit. We have the choice to limit or end contact with those who continue to not support our wellness. Let us put on the breastplate of righteousness and not be shaken by the negativity of others.

In Jesus's name, amen.
Daily reading: Romans 8:31

DAY 73

Affirmation

I express my emotions with love and kindness.

As I become in touch with who I am,
I am more and more aware
The conduct that produced stress
No longer appeals to me.
I am now a decider rather than a reactor,
Foreseeing the consequence before I act.

Meditation

Let us take the time to make conscious decisions about how we will conduct ourselves in all situations. As we develop spiritual awareness, we begin to see behavior patterns we have acquired that contributed to the stress in our lives. These survival traits are not in line with who we truly are. We can make better decisions about our behavior when we make it a practice to think first before we react. It can become our habit to look at all possible consequences of our behavior to help us make better decisions on how we will handle situations. Self-control is one of the fruits of the spirit. Let us ask God to develop this in us so we can be conscious deciders in life rather than overreactors.

In Jesus's name, amen.
Daily reading: 2 Peter 3:14–17 and Proverbs 25:28

DAY 74

Affirmation

*I allow myself the time and space to grieve
when grief surfaces from within.*

So busy blaming other things,
I miss the true culprit of my pain.
The cause of my grief is hidden deep,
Afraid of being found out,
Afraid of deeper pain.
Come out so I can see you, old friend,
Then send you on your way.

Meditation

Let us not be afraid to bring to the surface old wounds that keep us stuck. When we have unresolved pain, it can surface repeatedly in other areas of our lives. Grief that has been suppressed comes out misdirected. When we find ourselves feeling low and upset often or overreacting to normal life issues, we may be dealing with suppressed grief. Acknowledging feelings surrounding hurtful situations can help release pain that is hindering us from a peaceful life. We may have fragments of our soul/divine essence scattered and left stuck in experiences that were traumatic. We can call back those fragments as we recognize the voids within us. To move past these blocks, we must forgive anyone who is responsible for causing trauma in our lives. Once we see where we are holding on to pain, we can release all people involved from our judgments and give them over to God for his judgment. That is true forgiveness. Let us seek guidance from the Holy Spirit to deliver us from old wounds in need of healing and call back to ourselves all our soul fragments.

In Jesus's name, amen.
Daily reading: Matthew 16:26 and Psalm 23:3

DAY 75

Affirmation

I care for my needs joyfully.

As I keep my spirit nourished,
I am willing and able to nourish others.
Drawing first for myself will keep me strong;
It is the mark of a loving soul.

Meditation

Let us remember that it is not selfish to take good care of ourselves. It is a loving gift to those around us. When we nourish and care for all our needs, we can offer our love and attention to others. When we do not care well for ourselves, we become drained and needy. No matter how much we continue to give to others, when we are not giving to ourselves, the quality of our effort lacks, and resentments can build. Only loving and unconditional giving benefits anyone. When we give out of guilt or wanting to build ourselves up, it taints any good deed. Let us make time for our own needs before we give our attention to others.

In Jesus's name, amen.
Daily reading: Luke 16:15

DAY 76

Affirmation

My kindness is my deepest wisdom.

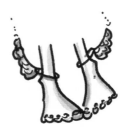

Treat the homeless like kings
And the prisoners like saints.
Offer love and compassion
Where others turn their backs,
And you will be the wise one
With blessings of peace.

Meditation

Let us never forget the importance of equality. We have all felt the impact of being looked down upon. It is a painful rejection that cuts deep into our hearts. It can shake up our feelings of self-worth and make us question who we are. No one ever deserves this type of treatment. People are worthy of love and respect no matter what their culture, social status, income, or upbringing. We are all children of God, wonderfully made. Let us always treat everyone as we wish to be treated. When we can accomplish that, we will have found true wisdom for which peace is the reward.

In Jesus's name, amen.
Daily reading: Hebrews 13:2

DAY 77

Affirmation

My faith is the power that transforms my life.

Time and again, I walk this same path,
Hoping it will lead me somewhere new.
But each time I end up in the same spot.

Meditation

Let us remember that our old behavior patterns will continue to produce the consequences they always have. Trying a new way is difficult for many of us; the familiar wins out over the unknown. Although we have done much inner work, old ways creep up unexpectedly at times. Some destructive behaviors are so ground in us that we may not even realize how negative they are. Behaviors we grew up watching and saw as normal can be extremely hard to change. We can reach out for support when we simply do not know how to overcome certain behaviors that go against the highest good. Sins like these can be cleansed from us when we pray to God for transformation and healing. Asking for deliverance from old ways will always be granted if we simply believe. Let us love ourselves enough to walk a new path, even when it feels uncomfortable, and break the cycle of outmoded behaviors.

In Jesus's name, amen.
Daily reading: 1 John 1:9

DAY 78

Affirmation

I see my goodness and beauty.

You say I am a beautiful earth angel.
What would it feel like if I believed you?
Today I will try to let it sink in.
I will be a beautiful earth angel today.

Meditation

Let us believe in the compliments we get from others. So many times, when nice things are said to us, we automatically reject them in our minds and see them as untrue. Who would we be if we believed how wonderful we are? How would we feel? We can allow ourselves to receive compliments as truth and be uplifted by them. That is the art of receiving, which is equally as important as the art of giving. We ruin the joy of these little gifts by rejecting them. God speaks to us in many ways and often through others. Let us practice the art of receiving and believing the uplifting encouragement that comes from others expressing the beauty they see in us.

In Jesus's name, amen.
Daily reading: Proverbs 27:17

DAY 79

Affirmation

I am careful to speak only in the direction of truth and love.

I must only speak words of truth.
Lies and gossip damage my spirit,
For when they pass through me,
My life force begins to drain away.
Negative intentions weaken my vitality.

Meditation

Let us be impeccable with our words. Speaking untruths or negatively toward or about others causes damage to ourselves. When we use our words to curse another, we are cursing ourselves. It drains the very life force we need to live peaceful, happy lives. Many of us are totally unconscious to this natural consequence, yet we feel the impact. Because our lives respond to our thoughts and intentions, it is natural that any negative words or intentions will draw back to us negative results. It is a law of the universe. When our intentions are to make others look or feel bad, we need to step back and correct ourselves. Let us care for our spiritual health by speaking only words of truth and sincerity.

In Jesus's name, amen.
Daily reading: James 3:10 and Genesis 12:3

DAY 80

Affirmation

I recognize when old programs creep up, and
I do the inner work to be free.

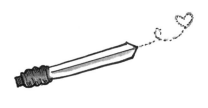

Why do I hide,
Afraid to face anyone
As if I'm in trouble?
I run from shame.

Meditation

Let us face the world with our heads held high. We may still feel the lingering imprint of shame from past unhealthy relationships. Growing up with constant criticism or someone putting us down can cause us to have deep-seeded shame that has manifested in our bodies. Acknowledging the presence of these feelings or false beliefs can start the healing process. We can call forth God's love to dissolve any shame or trauma still lingering within us. Sitting quietly and breathing in a steady rhythm will open us for the power of God's glory and love to enter and restore us back to God's light. We have the power to call this forth anytime with a simple request and belief in God's glory to heal us. Let us call forth God's love to melt away anything that hinders our highest good.

In Jesus's name, amen.
Daily reading: Ephesians 5:8 and 2 Corinthians 3:18

DAY 81

Affirmation

In my weakness, God's strength sustains me.

In this solemn darkness,
My life shattering before me,
Everything out of my control,
Too much to handle.
My body numb and lifeless,
My mind completely blank.
My spirit gently leaves me
To go and seek help.

Meditation

Let us remember that in our darkest moments, in times of trauma, divine intervention is always at hand. Angels surround us always and are called to work for our highest good. We can let go in our weak and battered state and rest knowing our spirits will always be strong and resourceful even when our minds and bodies are worn down to nothing. Our spirits are everlasting and will always live on in peace and love with God. It is our connection to a deeper truth and our higher purpose. We can trust our spirits to seek divine assistance on our behalf, even when we are unable. Let us trust the beautiful design of all beings of God's love and light to carry us through anything.

In Jesus's name, amen.
Daily reading: Psalm 91:11

DAY 82

Affirmation

I am love.

As I restore myself back to who I truly am,
Light illuminates things I could not see.
Beauty hidden by the darkness now shines bright.
Truth resonates with my heart.

Meditation

As we begin remembering our true selves, let our hearts be light with joy. We are restoring what life has weakened: our beautiful loving souls. As we walk our path of healing, we begin to see ourselves in a new light. What we once thought was hopeless no longer feels as overwhelming. God is rejoicing for us as we awaken from our slumber. We are beautiful and loving beings who have been tricked into thinking we are not enough. As we see more and more who we truly are, we can begin thriving as we were designed to and live out our purpose with passion for life. Let us acknowledge our beauty and strength as we rise into our divine true nature.

In Jesus's name, amen.
Daily reading: Luke 10:19 and 1 Peter 1:3

DAY 83

Affirmation

I honor my need for quiet space.

This sacred space of mine,
Just a small and cozy cubbyhole.
I declare it my sanctuary of peace,
A place to regroup and just be,
A place to cry and restore,
A place to visit with Holy Spirit,
A place that is only mine.

Meditation

Let us honor the value of having a sacred space that is all our own. When we designate a place where we can have solitude, it gives us a retreat from the world when we need it. We have embarked on a process of self-growth and healing, which is important work. Having a special place for our meditating, praying, journaling, reading, or crying, or just breathing, can make a big difference in our lives. We meet God in the secret place within us. Let us honor the sacred work we are doing by creating a safe space with no outside distractions to be alone with our Creator.

In Jesus's name, amen.
Daily reading: Matthew 6:6

DAY 84

Affirmation

I focus my loving attention where it is well received.

I will sever my ties from this situation
that drains the life from me.
For the precious energy expended on one
could be serving many,
Many who deserve my love.

Meditation

Let us not expend our emotional energy on those who constantly drain us with their stress. Those who choose to live in fear and who create chaos with others will suck the life right out of us. There are so many people deserving of our time, attention, and service. People who sincerely appreciate our efforts do not drain us—they sustain us. When one person depletes so much from us that we have nothing to give to those who deserve our assistance and love, we suffer greatly. May God guide us and give us strength and courage to free ourselves from drama and chaos. Let us lovingly and wisely direct our energy.

In Jesus's name, amen.
Daily reading: Isaiah 32:17–18

DAY 85

Affirmation

I know the angels are always with me.

This presence I feel is unmistakable now.
I know you well.
I don't see you; I just know.
I know you hold me close when I cry.
I know you rejoice when I laugh.
I know you love me tenderly for all I am.
And I know I love you with all of my heart.

Meditation

Let us be grateful for the presence of angels. Many of us have felt and come to know this presence well. We develop this fine-tune sense when we begin to trust and allow ourselves to believe in what we sense even when we do not see with our physical eyes. With so many miracles happening all around, it is hard to deny the fact that a mysterious, loving force resides among us. God works through the angels in many ways to help us. Let us fine-tune our senses through faith, always remembering to be grateful for our unseen friends and the blessings they bring.

In Jesus's name, amen.
Daily reading: Psalm 34:7

DAY 86

Affirmation

I live by the law of love.

All laws wiped out,
Replaced by one command:
Love thy neighbor as thyself.
What a simple, brilliant plan.
For if we truly love ourselves
And then our neighbors too,
Never could there be a crime,
For love would always rule.

Meditation

Let us live by the golden rule in all our affairs. It is such a genius idea. If everyone in the world followed this rule, there would be no crime. There would be no need for any laws because everything is encompassed in this one simple phrase: love thy neighbor as thyself. Before we act or make any decisions, we can ask ourselves, "Is this unloving toward anyone?" It is such an easy way to gauge our lives and keep us on track. Let us use this simple rule that Jesus has laid out for us to make wise choices.

In Jesus's name, amen.
Daily reading: James 2:8 and Colossians 3:12–14

DAY 87

Affirmation

The accuser has no power over me. I am free.

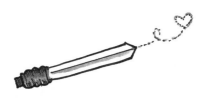

My deliverance is here.
Obstructions have been removed;
Unwanted influence has been shed.
My hopes and dreams can now unfold
With calm certainty that I am ready.

Meditation

Let us rejoice in our hard work toward becoming our true selves. So much in our lives has had to change to fit the person we were meant to be. When we strive for a better life, there is always work to be done. Resolution from old ways of living takes time and diligence on our part. The impact of living against our true nature causes many physical ailments due to the blocked energy of trapped emotions. As we have worked toward understanding how we have miscreated these problems in our lives, we also begin undoing the damage through our commitment to turn away from those old ways. We now are for ourselves rather than against. Our efforts will of course continue, yet we can feel a measure of safety now, knowing our hard work is paying off. Let us wholeheartedly embrace this new life filled with the fruits of the spirit and give thanks to God for all that is good.

In Jesus's name, amen.
Daily reading: 2 Thessalonians 3:3

DAY 88

Affirmation

I stay grounded in peace as I soar to new heights of success.

To measure my success, I carefully reflect.
I must look further than all of my achievements,
For they do not count anymore,
And my life experiences hold only a clue.
I look at who I have become due to those things.
There lies my true success.

Meditation

Let us remember where our true value lies. We know by now that our worth is not measured by our achievements or what we have in life. It is measured solely on who we have become because of these things. Have we become bitter from hardships, or do we take the loving route and let hardship strengthen our ability to be compassionate? Do we let our achievements give us a feeling of entitlement over others, or do we humble ourselves and offer love to those less fortunate? The experiences in our lives play a big part in shaping our character but do not define who we are. Our actions of love and kindness tell the story of our true success. By God's grace, all our life experiences can be used for our benefit now. Let us be among the successful by not collapsing ourselves in either the highs or the lows, but rather by striving for peacefulness in all we do.

In Jesus's name, amen.
Daily reading: James 3:18 and 2 Thessalonians 3:16

DAY 89

Affirmation

As I heal, so also is humanity healing.

What an honor to have the ability to love
Through this power we can heal the world,
To a state of joy no human has yet to feel.
Collective love will transform our existence
As more and more of humanity discovers it is time.

Meditation

Let us honor our innate ability to send and receive love. We must only have an open heart to access this gift. Our thoughts of love can transform our world with the power of Holy Spirit operating. When we direct our love to others, even across the globe, they certainly receive it. Love is an unseen power that travels wherever we tell it to. This is the power we were created from: God's love. When we have pure love for another, it is God loving through us. This beautiful gift can calm and comfort a loved one who is miles away. We can practice visualizing love as a gentle breeze or gust of wind traveling anywhere our thoughts direct it. In time, it will be second nature to send loving energy with only a quick passing thought guiding it. When more and more people begin accessing this ability, there will be a major shift in our world. Healing happens through the force of love. Let us practice sending love with our thoughts and keeping our hearts open to receiving it as well.

In Jesus's name, amen.
Daily reading: 1 Timothy 1:6 and Genesis 2:7

DAY 90

Affirmation

I allow God's love to transform my mind.

This knowledge is powerful,
But not enough
Until we can understand
It is useless information.

Meditation

Let us seek a deeper understanding of the power of love. To know that love is good and healing is important, but until we understand the depth of its ability, we are limited. It is the most crucial life force of our whole existence. It is the love of our Creator that made us, and it is also God's love that flows through us to others. Until we can see the absolute need to live with love toward everyone, the world as a whole will not have peace. The power of love will indeed heal the world, and it begins with everyone making a conscious decision to develop an attitude of love in all aspects of one's life. It can take time to unlearn the old ways, but it is the only option if we are to make our world a good place for future generations. Let us grow in our understanding of this powerful phenomenon through prayer and practice.

In Jesus's name, amen.
Daily reading: 1 Corinthians 13:13 and Philippians 2:13

DAY 91

Affirmation

One by one, the filters of distortion are dissolving.

I look upon the world with eyes of spirit,
Seeing only love.
My gaze looks beyond the mundane.
It looks beyond the flesh.
What a beautiful sight to see.

Meditation

Let us always see the goodness in ourselves and others. At the core, we are all creatures of spirit living in this mixed-up world. Our minds can get clouded by surface matters and seeming imperfection. We can look beyond the surface and see a deeper beauty to everyone when we practice being understanding and loving toward others. We can practice seeing through the eyes of God as we remain diligent in our healing and restoration. As we continually remove the filters of this world, the truth is more easily seen. Our distorted vision is clearing. What an amazing world this will be when all people spiritually wake up, restore, and live with God's love as the only driving force behind all we do. Problems will begin to melt away, and everyone will be cared for. Let our lives be a model to others of the joy of living in the presence of God's love and truth.

In Jesus's name, amen.
Daily reading: 3 John 1:4

DAY 92

Affirmation

I send healing love by my thoughts and prayers.

As a firsthand witness to heartbreak,
A helpless sadness engulfs you to the core
To see an innocent person be hurt
As a devastating turn of events unfold.
Knowing there will be a lasting impact,
You desperately try to soften the blow,
Praying your love can counter their pain.

Meditation

Let us know our love does indeed make a difference. Watching others go through painful life experiences can cause us to feel so helpless and even angry. Our loving instinct is to want to fix things and take away others' pain. A sense of powerlessness can overcome us and impact our own well-being. How do we separate enough to keep ourselves okay while at the same time being there for those going through heartache or trauma? By honoring our feelings as well as theirs and remembering the wise saying, "This too shall pass." We need to know that even though there are many things we cannot control, we are never powerless; the love we offer has great power. Love comforts, love heals, and love never fails because it is none other than God loving through us! Let us us use the power of love to offer strength and support to others.

In Jesus's name, amen.
Daily reading: John 16:22

DAY 93

Affirmation

Through God's grace, I can forgive.

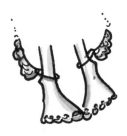

Let us give forgiveness
and lift each other high
through tender words and kindness,
wipe the tears we all may cry.

Meditation

Let us understand what it means to forgive. It is to offer grace to one who has done wrong to us. When we look at why forgiveness is so crucial, we see that by not forgiving, we harbor resentment. Resentment blocks us from peace and growth. Forgiveness comes through having compassion. We may wonder whether we are capable of compassion toward someone who has acted in an evil or cruel way. The answer is yes! We can find compassion by seeking out the truth behind the wrongdoing. When we truly take the time to contemplate this, we will always find that the wrongful act toward us has nothing really to do with us; it stems from a much deeper problem within them. When we realize that it is not personal but rather an emotional or spiritual sickness of the other person, we can let go of hurt feelings and understand the person's inner pain. This compassion is what precipitates forgiveness. It is what enables us to see them through loving eyes. Let us find peace by forgiving even the deepest hurts.

In Jesus's name, amen.
Daily reading: Luke 6:37 and Proverbs 10:12

DAY 94

Affirmation

I live in spirit and truth.

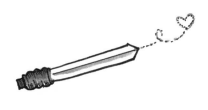

A tiny mustard seed,
Planted and nurtured
Over time, grows.
It becomes fruitful
And, with further nurturing,
Grows into maturity.
A strong tree and long limbs

Meditation

Let us look at this Bible story told by Jesus, the master at living in love. He said the kingdom of God was like a tiny mustard seed that grew over time with proper nurturing into a mature tree that could offer respite to others. The mustard seed is our initial faith and desire to live in spirit and love. When this desire is nurtured through seeking spiritual growth, over time we reach spiritual maturity. Those who are spiritually mature have mastered the art of living in the presence of God, in constant communion with him. The kingdom of God exudes from them; they live in it. They are the mature tree that can offer us shade and rest and rejuvenate us. As we decide to walk with Jesus, the mustard seed of faith within us will grow. Let us nurture it daily by learning and studying all we can about Jesus's great wisdom. The kingdom of God is the realm in which God's will is fulfilled. We can live in this kingdom by seeking to live God's will for us here on Earth. His will is for us to live in love for ourselves and others and to have prosperity and abundance in every aspect of our lives. Let us patiently strive to grow in spirit and gain the fruits that come with that: love, joy, peace, long suffering, kindness, goodness, faith, mildness, and self-control.

In Jesus's name, amen.
Daily reading: Matthew 13:31–32

DAY 95

Affirmation

I trust my heart to discern what is true.

Barriers of mistrust
built up by religious shame.
Fears invoked by elders.
Twisted teachings
to control the masses.
Misused power kept hidden.
So many people shaken to the core
by the corruption of truth,
now floundering, unable to trust.

Meditation

Let us break down the barriers of protection we have built up due to strict fear- and shame-based religious experiences from our past. We are now safe to decide for ourselves what truth is. We need not shudder and run from the things that remind us of past unpleasant experiences. If we grew up being shamed for things that are basic human nature, or scolded for questioning the teachings we were taught, we may find ourselves wanting to block out anything that sounds even slightly religious. Our walls may be extremely high. Let us remember that God's love is the ultimate truth. We can look back and be grateful for all the difficult times, knowing they have brought us to where we are now. We now live amid God's love and relish the blessings all the more for having lived through hardship. Let us take down the walls built up for survival, knowing we are now safe in the hands of God's divine love!

In Jesus's name, amen.
Daily reading: 2 John 1:7–11

DAY 96

Affirmation

*I now can search the deepest part of my being and
shine the light of love in every fiber.*

As I stumble over and over
On the same bumps,
Even when I quickly smooth the surface,
Always the bumps reappear.
So now I shall dig deep,
I will find what keeps pushing
Its way back through.
I will finally take the time
And put forth the effort
To uncover the source of my shame.
Only then will I truly see
What has hindered my healing.

Meditation

Let us take the time to contemplate what still causes us lingering shame. Although our spirits may be renewed by the choice to abide in love, our minds need time to be fully cleansed as we learn this new way of living. One of the toughest and quite common sources of deep-rooted shame for many of us is sexual in nature. Sexual shame from past experiences, behaviors and thoughts cause too many people unbearable pain. When we are hindered from peace because of these kinds of memories or thoughts, it is time to look at the root cause. We can safely allow ourselves to look back with loving eyes and have compassion for ourselves. Even wrong choices and unhealthy behaviors sexual in nature have an underlying cause that we can piece together without shameful judgment on ourselves. We can uncover these things and forgive ourselves. We deserve forgiveness no matter what! This may be an uncomfortable part of our healing journey, yet it is the most powerful when we can finally recognize, understand, and forgive. Let us uncover the deepest hurts with our eyes wide open and seeing with love the things that once brought shame. Loving forgiveness is the answer. May we offer that to ourselves now and forever!

In Jesus's name, amen.
Daily reading: Romans 8:1

DAY 97

Affirmation

My heart's desires are manifesting.

I will pray.
I will ask.
I will believe.
I will listen.
I will be shown.
I will receive.

Meditation

Let us remember to ask our Creator to help us fulfill the desires of our hearts. The deep-down desire of all of us is ultimately for peace—peace within ourselves, peace for our families, and peace for all of humanity. Prayers are made with faith that they are heard and will be answered. The key is faith: we must have total belief. Our faith grows over time as we see the way God has answered our prayers. We begin to see the power that comes from affirming our requests before they even manifest. Amen means "so be it." We are decreeing that it has already taken place after we pray. We are casting blessings as we attach faith to our requests. Let us believe with all our hearts and souls that our prayers are answered perfectly.

In Jesus's name, amen.
Daily reading: James 1:6 and 1 John 5:14

DAY 98

Affirmation

Truth has set me free.

I must stay centered in truth,
even when it is painful,
only speaking with love
so that all that is dark
transcends into beautiful light.

Meditation

Let us remember to put on the full armor of God every day. The wise words of the apostle Paul teach us everything we need to transform our lives, and collectively our world, into a state of love and peace. He describes putting on the belt of truth, the body armor of righteousness, the shoes of peace, the shield of faith, and the sword of the Holy Spirit or word of God. We can gently remind ourselves before we begin each day that these are the only tools we need for a life of peace. Are we honest with others and ourselves? Do we continually make a conscious effort to do the right and most loving thing? Do we know that our words have the power to lift others up or to tear them down? Do we walk through the world in peace with all our brothers and sisters? Do we keep our faith strong through prayer and meditation? Lastly, do we stand firm and believe in God's law of love? Let us all take an honest look at ourselves and only ourselves and take responsibility for our roles in the world. We need not worry about anyone else's choices and behaviors because focusing on our own is enough. We can lead by example as we work toward bettering ourselves. Let us study the wise council that has been gifted to us and put on our full armor each day. Let us all grow together in harmony and support each other as we transform our world into a loving home for all.

In Jesus's name, amen.
Daily reading: 1 Corinthians 11:1

DAY 99

Affirmation

My roots run to the beginning of time.

My roots run deep,
hidden yet sustaining my very existence.
But my branches stretch far into the sky
for all to see and enjoy.
Beauty beyond words,
love beyond understanding,
This beautiful family of mine!

Meditation

Let us celebrate the hidden forces of life sustaining power we receive from our family past and present. No words can even describe the mystical wonder of family bonds. We can even feel the deep ties of our ancestors and the impact of their existence on our very own. A special connection runs through family genes that teach us unconditional love. Even when there are disputes or distance between us and family members, that divine love remains. It keeps us connected, nourishing us through energies only seen through spiritual eyes. With each deliverance we receive and every lie we conquer, we impart these healings to our entire bloodline of generations past and in the future. We can trace our roots even further than the family we call our own and at some point, every person will end up in the same family tree in the beginning of time. We can marvel at the idea that we are all family here on this earth. Let us cherish the family we are blessed to share our life with and honor all families knowing we all come from the same divine love.

In Jesus's name, amen.
Daily reading: 1 Timothy 5:1–2

DAY 100

Affirmation

My sacred heart is fully open.

Closing my eyes,
Slowly I breath in,
Slowly I breath out,
Filling my heart space
With the most precious gift,
An element so precise
It sustains all that is alive
And activates the divine sacred heart
Hidden deep within us all.

Meditation

Let us realize the power of our breath. How we breathe is as important as how we eat. When we are anxious and stressed, our breath gets shorter and more labored, causing our bodies to strain to get the oxygen it needs. Slowing our breathing calms us. When Jesus spoke his sermons, he often ended them by saying, "He who has ears to hear, let him hear" (Matthew 11:15 ESV). He was speaking of not physical auditory hearing—he was talking about spiritual hearing, our inner knowing or inner sense of intuition. Some may call it our sixth sense. Whatever you chose to call it, it is a very real gift for those who live from the heart. Living from the heart is about loving all without condition. We must develop this and train ourselves to live from the heart. Our breath can connect us to this ability. We can take time each day to practice slow breathing to quiet our minds so we can hear God speak to our hearts. Meditation is the practice of quieting our mind and opening our hearts to hear with our spiritual ears. With practice, we can learn to live in this state of Christ consciousness. Let us take time each day to focus our breathing into our hearts and familiarize ourselves with this sense of calmness. We are living in a world that is purging the old to begin living in a new way, a loving way. Let us help all of humanity by evolving individually, using our breath to breathe in the love coming to us now from the heavens.

In Jesus's name, amen.
Daily reading: Job 27:3–4 and Job 33:4

DAY 101

Affirmation

I live from my heart, where God whispers all I need to know.

Your heart was made to love and guide,
Your mind to create and solve.
Your body to build and make,
And a vessel for the spirit
To disperse love, joy, and peace.

Meditation

Let us honor and trust the Holy Spirit within us to lead us through a life of wonder and fulfillment. When we follow our loving heart, where God's Holy Spirit resides, things go smoothly and feel in order. The Holy Spirit knows more than we ever consciously could. Our pure and open hearts sense the subtle voice of the Holy Spirit. Yet most of us are not used to letting our hearts guide us. We are trained to use our heads to lead us when that was never the intended design. Our minds carry memory and fears and try to use logic in guiding us. These things are wonderful for implementing plans but do not have access to all the necessary information to make big decisions. It is through our hearts that God speaks. We may think we need to understand all the decisions we chose, yet we never could. We must have faith in God to know what we cannot see. We must be still and trust that all things work for the good for those who love God and seek him. When we go against God's will, we feel friction and distress rather than peace. We can train ourselves to live in spirit through practice. Making a conscious decision to let our lives be guided by the Holy Spirit is a gentle way of living that has unlimited rewards beyond our wildest dreams. May we all tap into this divine gift and begin to live with more ease.

In Jesus's name, amen.
Daily reading: Ephesians 6:17 and Romans 8:9

DAY 102

Affirmation

I will be still and know.

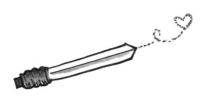

What does your heart say?
Your heart already knows.
Listen with your spiritual ears;
There the truth is shown.

Meditation

Let us remember the purpose of our spiritual eyes and ears. They are our navigation system through life that uses our hearts to give us messages. We can trust them to guide us. When faced with decisions, let us go first to our hearts, not our minds. Our minds are cluttered with outside information. When our hearts are pure and stay true to God's will for us, they speak to us through our spiritual senses. We can begin to use our innate wisdom for all life's decisions by going within. Before we make any big decision, let us sit quietly by ourselves and focus on our breathing until we feel calm. Then we can ask God to speak to our hearts and notice our feelings as we think of each option we could choose. What do we feel when we think of the different options? The one that brings us a sense of peace or feels right is our answer. We must remember that the right choice may not logically seem right to others, but our hearts are connected to God, who sees the big picture. We can trust this even when it defies logic. May we all open our hearts where God's perfect love reigns.

In Jesus's name, amen.
Daily reading: John 8:47 and Isaiah 30:21

DAY 103

Affirmation

The belt of truth is buckled around my waist.

As I rise into my personal power
through standing in truth,
I am set free from the bondage of deception.

Meditation

May we always remember the power we have when we live in truth. Truth resonates on high frequencies. Falsehoods resonate in the lower vibratory range. God resides in the highest of frequencies, in the light of love, and as we live in truth, we remain close to God where we are our authentic selves. The world has operated in darkness, where there is chaos and heartache. We are choosing to raise our vibration through living in the light of truth. As we live this way, we are sending out high vibrations of love that heal those around us. May we be diligent in seeking out our hearts for what is good and true and live in the light of God's love.

In Jesus's name, amen.
Daily reading: Proverbs 30:5

DAY 104

Affirmation

I have the breastplate of righteousness in place.

My mind lies in wait
for the direction of my heart.
From my heart, loving right action flows,
keeping my heart safe and sound.

Meditation

Let us remember to keep our hearts protected by making sure all our actions are loving. Righteousness is our only true protection from heartache. Being righteous is about having good intent and no hidden agenda. It also encompasses purity. When we polarize toward the light of God's love, we purify our hearts. When we act out of love, we are sending out vibrations that uplift others. We are allowing God's love to flow through us. Love heals all things with its divine power. It can restore any darkness back into light. When we contemplate what right action would be in any given situation, we can go within our hearts and make sure our intentions are pure and good. We now know the importance of loving pure intent. We know our very life depends on it. We create a life of peace and joy using this fruit of the spirit. May we always remember the power we have from acting with love and goodness.

In Jesus's name, amen.
Daily reading: Isaiah 33:15–17

DAY 105

Affirmation

I allow the hidden to rise to be released.

When something said to me
triggers pain to well up inside,
and feelings of rejection come to the surface,
I have come far enough now to not react.
For I know it is time to quietly search myself
for the lie hidden deep within
and adjust my mindset to
align with truth.

Meditation

We have come far enough now to notice when hidden lies come up to the surface for healing. As we progress, we are seeing how many layers we still need to peel away that do not line up with truth. When someone says something that produces unpleasant feelings, we now know it is not truly about what is being said. It has simply brought up something within us from which we need deliverance. Old lies are hidden deep within us. Many of the lies do not come up until we are in situations that are like the original circumstances that caused the lie to seed and take root. Thankfully, we can trace back these old unhealthy mindsets, and we now have the tools to rip them out from the root. As we quietly go in contemplation and ask ourselves where these feelings truly come from, we allow the mystery to unravel. We allow the original pain to be seen and felt for what it really is: a lie we have believed and allowed to control our minds. We can then go in prayer simply asking for deliverance. We can allow the truth to lock into our minds so we can be free. Deep-seeded fear, abandonment, rejection, or shame programming can finally be removed for good and be replaced with the truth of our incredible worth and goodness. Let us remember that through Christ, we can heal anything when we allow the deepest truth to be seen.

In Jesus's name, amen.
Daily reading: John 14:26

DAY 106

Affirmation

I am a mighty spiritual warrior.

I believe in myself
as the warrior I am,
knowing I am fighting for the collective
and the generations yet to come.

Meditation

We must keep our faith so strong at this point. If we have made it this far, we are powerful spiritual warriors. As we clear out old programming within ourselves, we are also clearing it for future generations. Just as we have inherited the lies and strong holds of the generations before us, so too will the ones to come inherit from us. As we are doing this work, we are not just working on what we have accumulated in our lifetime. Our work is much deeper than that. We have taken on the task of clearing our ancestors' programming as well. We can hold our heads high knowing we have a strong army behind us in the heavenly places. Let us have faith that the path we are paving for those to come is a true legacy of love.

In Jesus's name, amen.
Daily reading: Ezekiel 18:2

DAY 107

Affirmation

I allow God's spirit to guide me to unusual places.

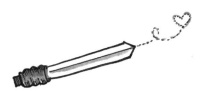

How could I have ever known
to be in this exact place
at this exact time
and find the exact person
that would overfill my heart
with love so sweet?

Meditation

Let us be filled with awe at how the Holy Spirit leads us when we are living in a partnership with God. When we allow ourselves to remain open to anything that is set before us, even when it defies all logic, we begin to witness miracles so incredible that it blows our minds. The Holy Spirit is so tangible to us now and will become more and more apparent in every moment of our lives. We are aligning ourselves with God as we continue releasing the old programs that use to control us. We are free to be the instruments of God's loving power that we were always meant to be. Our innate design is to be conduits of the powerful force of God's love. As we draw closer to God, we move into harmony with his perfect love. What a beautiful song we create when our lives are a symphony of peace and harmony! Let us remain in the glory of God by continuing to keep ourselves open to the mysterious ways of God's love.

In Jesus's name, amen.
Daily reading: Revelation 4:1–11

DAY 108

Affirmation

I call forth God's love and protection around my mind.

As I reach new heights,
I become a target of dark forces.
They know that a powerful warrior is being equipped
and that many will soon be saved from them.

Meditation

We must diligently pray for the protection of our minds at this point in our journey. As we get stronger, we will be seen as a threat to those still operating in darkness. We have realized by now that the mind is the battlefield of the world. We are turned against ourselves by the infiltration of deceit all around us that can easily put us back into fear. We have the tools now to keep ourselves safe from the tactics of the dark forces operating in the world. The helmet of salvation is our safeguard. As we pray and walk in truth and love, our helmets stay intact. God's love and spirit is stronger and more powerful than anything that could ever come at us. Yet it is up to us to remain in the presence of God. Let us put on our helmets each day by prayerful declarations that Jesus is our King and by walking in his ways of peace.

In Jesus's name, amen.
Daily reading: 2 Peter 1:3 and Matthew 19:26.

DAY 109

Affirmation

I reside in the realm of God's love and righteousness.

From my heart radiates the love of God.
An ocean of golden light that surrounds me,
It bathes me in living water.
It cleanses my soul and purifies my body.
It keeps me on the path of divine beauty
And connects me to all that is good.

Meditation

How blessed we are to have found our way home! Through our conscious decision to heal, we have returned to our hearts. The beauty we can see now is astounding. Even when life is challenging and we catch only glimpses of God's perfect plan, we have the knowledge that we are always in the presence of his love. At any moment, we can adjust our focus and see the goodness all around; we know how to do that now. We know how to remain in this realm through our diligent efforts to keep putting on the breastplate of righteousness. What a relief to know this is not our own righteousness—it is the righteousness of God that we could never have on our own. Let us express our gratitude for all the goodness we have access to when we stay close to God and seek to know the righteous ways of his heart.

In Jesus's name, amen.
Daily reading: Romans 5:1–5

DAY 110

Affirmation

God's peace lives in me.

May all the Earth know God's peace.
May all the hearts be filled with it.
May all the feet walk in it.

Meditation

Let us remember that peace is ours simply by keeping our faith strong. The power of believing that anything is possible through Christ rewards us with the gift of peace. As we are filled with peace beyond understanding, we radiate joy onto others. How amazing that the inner work we have done can benefit those around us with no effort on our part. We can expect others to notice something is different about us. We should also expect that others will want what we have. Let us extend our peace by being guiding lights and sharing with those who are drawn into our lives. We can spread the peace of God simply by our example, but we can go even further by our willingness to teach and guide those whom God sends our way. The true joy comes when we see others find what we have! May we keep our hearts open to opportunities to share God's peace to everyone who seeks.

In Jesus's name, amen.
Daily reading: Romans 15:13 and Psalm 119:165

DAY 111

Affirmation

I chose to reside in the kingdom of God.

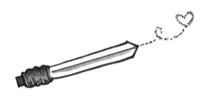

Side by side they exist,
The old Earth and the new,
Resonating opposite of each other.
The new Earth is of unity, love, and truth.
The old Earth is of separation, fear, and falsehoods.
It is a simple choice of which one we choose to abide in.

Meditation

Let us comprehend the power of how we have chosen to live. The kingdom of God is here, and Jesus is the King. We are now living in it and have love, peace, and joy. We made the choice to live according to our true nature and abide in the presence of God. We have embarked on a profound healing and found out that our spirits are guided by God. We know that when our thoughts are aligned with love, the power of God's love flows through us. We continue to train ourselves to hold loving thoughts, and thus God's miraculous essence flows through us. It has brought us perfect love in return as we resonate to the highest of energies. We are learning how to operate as we were designed to. We are learning the intended use of our bodies, which is to be in submission to our minds. The intended use of our minds is to be in submission to our spirits. The intended use of our spirits is to be in submission to God so his perfect will guides us. The intended use of our hearts is where God navigates us. We are learning how to use each part of our perfectly designed selves to live as God planned. We are becoming familiar with living in spirit and truth. The veil between the spirit world and humanity is thinned for those who choose God's love. How amazing it is to have the option to live with no impossibilities. May God guide us in helping others as we continue in our own restoration.

In Jesus's name, amen.
Daily reading: Revelation 21:1–7

Never forget:

BEautiful **YOU**

Our God in Heaven,

Thank you for continuing to guide our path of healing and restoration so we can help others. We pray that you continue revealing more and more of your mysteries to us as we are ready to comprehend. Help us to remember that what we put our focus and attention on will be our master. Help our minds' eye to be firmly set on your truth, righteousness, faith, peace, and spirit as the remedy to overcome the world. May we overcome fear as we abide in your love. May we boldly declare your truth where there are falsehoods. May our bodies, minds, hearts, and spirits be at ease and in perfect harmony with themselves and with you, radiating your healing love everywhere we go.

Help us be the salt of the earth and the light of the world!

We give you all the praise and glory for the work you are doing in our lives. We pray that your perfect will be done, that your name be praised, and that your word would not return void!

In Jesus's mighty name, amen.

About the Author

Rachelle Kinney is a prophetic writer and holistic healer from St. Paul, Minnesota. She began her studies of the healing arts in 2003 with a focus on holistic healing, and she has worked with many healing modalities over the years. She has a deep passion for prophetic intercession as well as healing and deliverance ministry, and her desire to see humanity heal drives her life. Rachelle began writing prophetically at the age of seventeen; her writings center around spiritual healing. The meditations in this book were originally given to her through the Holy Spirit to assist in her own sacred healing. Having gone through a seven-year healing and restoration period, she was inspired to share what was gifted to her. She also does work in home health care. She brings her experience in healing to help her clients have quality of life, while remaining in their home environment. Rachelle enjoys the blessing of frequent time spent with her grandchildren.